MASTERING BUSINESS STYLE

You can make a lasting impression on clients and colleagues—and pave the way for a successful career—with this essential guide to business etiquette and office protocol. You'll discover:

- The time-honored results of good etiquette
- Secrets to a successful lunch or dinner meeting
- How to choose a restaurant for business
- How to respond to invitations
- When to accept or decline a business gift
- Appropriate telephone manners
- Tips for proper letter writing
- Your business wardrobe: dressing to make a statement
- How etiquette boosts personal confidence
- Business in foreign lands: playing by different rules
- Gift-giving in other countries
- The right way to greet, introduce, and shake hands
- How to become the consummate executive diplomat
- Everyday office protocol
  . . . AND MUCH MORE!

THE TOTAL MANAGEMENT PROGRAM FOR THE 1990s!
From the National Institute of Business Management

THIS REMARKABLE NEW SERIES INCLUDES:

MASTERING MEETINGS
MASTERING OFFICE POLITICS
MASTERING DECISION MAKING
MASTERING BUSINESS WRITING
MASTERING BUSINESS STYLE

THE ESSENTIAL KEYS TO SUCCESS FOR TODAY'S MANAGERS

MASTERING BUSINESS STYLE

National Institute of Business Management

Previously published as *Mastering Business Etiquette and Protocol*

BERKLEY BOOKS, NEW YORK

Previously published as *Mastering Business Etiquette and Protocol.*

This Berkley book contains the complete text
of the original edition. It has been
completely reset in a typeface designed
for easy reading and was printed from new film.

MASTERING BUSINESS STYLE

A Berkley Book / published by arrangement with
National Institute of Business Management, Inc.

PRINTING HISTORY
National Institute of Business Management, Inc. edition / March 1989
Berkley trade paperback edition / November 1991

ISBN: 0-425-13040-1

A BERKLEY BOOK® TM 757,375
Berkley Books are published by The Berkley Publishing Group,
200 Madison Avenue, New York, New York 10016.
The name "BERKLEY" and the "B" logo
are trademarks belonging to Berkley Publishing Corporation.

PRINTED IN THE UNITED STATES OF AMERICA

10 9 8 7 6 5 4 3 2 1

Contents

1

Introduction

For manners are not idle, but the fruit
Of loyal nature and of noble mind.
         GUINEVERE
     —Alfred Lord Tennyson

A mastering of the social graces is especially important to the man or woman who wants to attain and maintain success in today's rapidly changing, fast-paced business world.

Now more than ever before

Why now, more than ever before? There are three good reasons:

One, we have already advanced into the high-technology years. The need for sensitive high-touch activity to counterbalance impersonal treatment and respond to human needs has become a reality.

Two, the business world has fewer boundaries, bringing together people from all parts of the globe to engage in business on a regular basis. Not only do individuals from foreign lands assemble to cooperate in person, but a stream of communication also requires that steps be taken to maintain a smooth flow of ideas, free from social misunderstandings that may offend, delay, or prevent bringing a business goal to a successful conclusion.

Three, women have eased into all areas of the business community, making it necessary to discard some of the old rules and establish new guidelines for behavior.

And finally, a fourth reason: According to Letitia Baldrige, well-known expert on the subject of etiquette with long service in the Diplomatic Corps and three years as Director of Staff for Mrs. Kennedy in the White House, "A flood of executives in their twenties, thirties and early forties were not trained in manners...comportment... [or]...in the nuances of relating to fellow human beings because we had the youth revolution, the women's revolution and...everybody doing his or her own thing. So as a result, there's been a breakdown at the family level and, of course, divorce doesn't help. Children have not been taught in the normal course of things. Young executives and even middle-aged executives are feeling awkward and ill at ease at not knowing exactly what is expected [of them]." Baldrige observes that senior executives who were trained in the old school with the old traditions are interested to know why somebody thirty-eight years old, who graduated from Harvard Business School, doesn't know any better.

Time-honored results

Now, as always, if you know what to do and how to do it with grace and style, you'll maintain a competitive edge that will follow you everywhere. Mastering and practicing business etiquette gives you an edge when you are considered for employment or advancement. It may even influence the initial salary proposal the company extends.

As you deal with subordinates, associates, and superiors, you're more likely to earn their favor and cooperation by observing the niceties that encourage a positive response from others.

When you brush up on, and stay abreast of, accepted etiquette skills, you enhance your success rate in getting an order, gaining a client, and keeping a customer. Suppliers and those you may depend upon in a pinch usually come through for you. You win favor by putting that something extra into your way of doing business.

4

Doing what comes naturally

One might assume that a successful individual has already mastered the "Art of Business Etiquette" and need not give the subject further consideration. However, changing times and social values challenge personal conduct. Doing what comes naturally does not prepare anyone to rise to all occasions. It's unlikely that all employees will represent the company in the best light if left to do what comes naturally.

Keen competition in the marketplace has prompted some firms to improve customer relations by establishing training programs that stress how to extend courteous service to customers. This has led to an increased number of seminars and courses on business etiquette. Etiquette consultants are now engaged for high-ranking company officials and first-line service employees. Executives recognize that mastering the art of business etiquette is vital to overall business achievement.

What exactly is business etiquette?

If you were able to question all the experts to be found, you would likely elicit a slightly different explanation from each one of them.

Terms and phrases like social graces, grace and style, niceties, courteous service, standards governing behavior, and acceptable procedure help to give a sense of the subject.

Still, your own appreciation of business etiquette depends upon two considerations, namely where and when.

The codes of conduct relative to business interaction in Japan or China differ from those in New York or California. Within the United States, what is acceptable in Philadelphia might be considered offensive in Atlanta.

Putting geographic differences aside, an older person might be offended by a gesture that would go unnoticed by a younger person. The titles Ms. and Mrs., or use of a first name, will antagonize some people, while others will find the informal form of address suitable.

And so it goes. The slightly elusive nature of the subject is the strongest argument for the need to pay attention to business etiquette, and to reinforce your skills in it.

What about protocol?

A dictionary definition of protocol is: "A code of diplomatic or military etiquette and precedence." For example, rules of protocol guide executives who oversee the display of the flag of The United States of America. Certain rules and customs prevail when displaying our flag both inside and outside of buildings and alongside other flags. At conferences, dedications, and various business gatherings, executives must adhere to guidelines that dictate the order in which the National Anthem and other musical tributes are to be performed. Numerous questions of protocol may arise when your firm hosts a formal dinner. These include seating arrangements, the proper sequence for making introductions, acknowledgment of government officials and dignitaries in attendance, and the correct use of titles like The Honorable. These and many other established rules should be observed in order to demonstrate respect for our nation and those with whom we come in contact.

Executives who plan functions and represent their companies at them risk embarrassment and misunderstanding when they are unaware of the rules of protocol.

A dollars-and-cents evaluation

Throughout the business day, the question of whether a business action is cost-effective is a legitimate and necessary question. Accordingly, it makes good business sense to determine the dollars-and-cents ramifications of correct business etiquette and protocol.

A Washington market research firm, Technical Assistance Research Programs Inc., conducted a study for the White House Office of Consumer Affairs that turned up figures you can use to calculate some of the cost of discourtesy to a business. One such figure states that "96% of unhappy customers never complain about discourtesy, but up to 91% will not buy again from the business that offended them. In addition, the average unhappy customer will tell his or her story to at least nine other people, and 13% of unhappy customers will tell more than 20 people."

Consider your own response, for example, to a discourteous supplier. You would probably take your business elsewhere, too. And, if you must continue to deal with the offensive party for reasons beyond your control, the relationship is strained. You are ready to sever business dealings at the first opportunity.

Moreover, you're likely to tell others about your unhappy experience. As Letitia Baldrige comments, "A company becomes a company you want to do business with because of the people who work in it, so it [business etiquette] has a very definite relationship to the bottom line."

2

Savoir-Faire Graces the Successful Breakfast, Lunch, or Dinner Meeting

No matter where a business meeting takes place, a certain amount of preplanning is necessary to enable you to see the occasion through to its desired conclusion.

First things first

The first question to ask yourself when you are the host or hostess is: What is the purpose of the meeting?

You may have to interview a job candidate, entertain a visiting client, talk to regional sales managers about introducing a new product line, or bounce a new idea off a colleague. Taking a moment to fix the purpose in your mind will enable you to make the appropriate advance arrangements.

One of the things that sets a mealtime meeting apart from most other meetings is that all five senses are in attendance at these gatherings. You'll want to keep sight, hearing, taste, touch, and smell in mind when making your plans, using each one to your best advantage.

Choosing the best place to meet

The setting you select to meet a promising job candidate will probably be different from the one you choose to entertain a visiting client. And your choice of meeting place, whether the firm's executive dining room, a famous eatery in a big city, or a private country club, could influence the outcome of the meeting.

Here are some points to consider:

- **Noisy or quiet?** There are times when you want a quiet setting so that all assembled can converse and be heard easily. This would be best, for example, when meeting with the regional sales staff. If, on the other hand, a male executive were meeting a female job candidate and he arranged the meeting in a quiet, intimate hideaway, the meeting place would not be appropriate. An out-of-town client might enjoy a dinner meeting at a lively well-known location. You display consideration for your guests when you consider the noise level of the meeting place.

- **Formal or relaxed?** A formal setting should set the tone for a more serious get-together. When you want to sound out a junior executive about considering a move to the West Coast to assume new responsibilities, a crystal and linen breakfast, with several servers attending the table, lends an air of importance to the meeting. On the other hand, meeting for a buffet lunch after a game of golf at the country club sets up a less serious forum for sounding out the same young executive. Your skill at selecting a location that visibly demonstrates the importance of the meeting should not go unnoticed.

- **Plain or fancy food?** Whether you are a fast-food fancier or a gourmet who dines regularly on French cuisine, when you set the mealtime meeting place it's important that you consider the food preferences of your guest(s). If a party you're meeting is only a telephone voice to you, you might ask him or her to suggest one or two places to meet. Even if you swing the meeting place to one you select, you should pick up a clue as to your guest's food preferences. There's little point in inviting a confirmed vegetarian to the city's finest steak house.

The meeting is likely to be strained if your guest finds little, if anything, to select after the salad has been served. If you know that a colleague is partial to good seafood, by all means invite him or her to join you at a seafood restaurant, remembering to select one that fits the criteria that will enable you to guide the meeting through to a successful conclusion. People are flattered when you remember their preferences.

Six ways to put your guest(s) at ease

More often than not, you will want to make your guests comfortable and put them at ease when you meet. (Of course, there are times when a dining-room meeting is designed to keep a guest less than relaxed.)

1. **Be precise about the time and place to meet.** When you arrange the meeting, be precise about directions. If you want to meet at the *bar* of The Great Bistro, remember to say so. Otherwise, your guest may wait in the foyer wondering what's keeping you, while you are at the bar wondering the same about your guest. If you are precise about where to meet, needless anxiety will be avoided.

   Plan to arrive for your meeting a few moments ahead of your guest(s). A good host or hostess should be there to greet the guest(s). If you find, at the last moment, that you're going to be unavoidably detained, call ahead to the restaurant or club, talk to someone with authority, ask that your guests be greeted and advised that you will be detained briefly. Leave instructions for them to be seated at your table and invited to have drinks.

   Even if your guests prefer to wait for your arrival before going to the table, this gracious gesture will minimize the impact of your tardiness. When you arrive, an apology is in order. Later, in private, remember to thank the restaurant representative who interceded for you. If it was the captain or maitre d', you can express your thanks with a gratuity.

2. **How to recognize a guest you've never seen before.** Trying to pick out a person from a telephone description can prove awkward. You can avoid this situation by arriving earlier than your guest, taking your table and alerting the captain or maitre d' that you are waiting for Ms. Jones. When she arrives, she will be shown to your table.

   If this is not convenient, you may wish to arrange to have Ms. Jones come to your office. Ms. Jones will announce herself to the receptionist or secretary and you will be able to travel together to the restaurant or club.

   Should it be necessary to meet in a crowded place, suggest a spot that is both secure and comfortable. A well-appointed hotel lobby can serve as a meeting place. Give detailed information. "I have a moustache and am six feet tall. I'll be wearing an all-weather coat. I'll wait for you near the gold clock on the Park Avenue side of the lobby." Your guest will feel more confident about finding you without the anxiety of approaching the wrong person.

3. **Take charge of the seating arrangements.** When some of your guests do not know others, or when junior executives are invited to a mealtime meeting with senior members of the firm, some of the group may hesitate about choosing a seat. You can put everyone at ease by directing each guest to an appropriate chair. Give the seating arrangements some advance thought, especially if those assembled number more than four. There are no foolproof, preset rules to follow here. Let the purpose of the meeting guide you in making the appropriate arrangements.

4. **What will you have to drink?** For a multitude of reasons, many people don't care to order an alcoholic beverage at a business meeting. Some will only order if you do. Sometimes, if they order an alcoholic beverage first and you don't, they feel uncomfortable. When you don't know your guests well, you can forestall anyone's qualms by announcing to the server, "I'll have white wine, please," and turning to your guests for their choices. One executive reveals that she orders an alcoholic beverage without exception. She may not drink it, but she orders it. She believes her guests are more comfortable that way.

5. **Guests should know that they are "guests."** Some mealtime meetings are set up in such a matter-of-fact fashion that although you take charge of the arrangements, your guest does not realize that he or she is, in fact, a guest. If you want to avoid a clumsy scene but you're not sure if the host/guest relationship is fully understood, you can arrange to have the check given directly to you. A private word to the captain or waiter in advance of being seated should be sufficient.

6. **Remember, there is a beginning and an end.** Mealtime meetings can occasionally stretch on with little regard for the clock. Sometimes, the servers move too slowly. Be aware of everyone's time restraints. If you have limited time to devote to the meeting, make your plans known in advance. When someone has a plane to catch, is expected back at the office, or must catch the last train home, be sure that you, as the host or hostess, are sensitive to their situations.

When your guest has special dietary requirements

Your guest's special dietary requirements should be considered when you plan the meeting. Still, once you learn of special needs, how should you proceed? Most diet restrictions can be accommodated without too much fuss. Some common dietary practices include:

- Maintaining a kosher diet, where milk and meat dishes would not be consumed at the same meal. In addition, shellfish would not be acceptable, nor would pork, nor would meat that has not been readied following strict guidelines. If your guest follows a strict kosher regimen, he or she may prefer not to meet when food is served. However, many businesspeople who maintain a kosher diet will dine at establishments that cater to their dietary requirements. It's best to ask your guest about his or her regimen in advance of the meeting. When you advise a chef well before the meeting, unusual requests may be satisfied with a minimum of fuss.

- Not all vegetarians follow the same dietary regimen. Here, too, it is best to ask about specific preferences in advance. A personal secretary may be sufficiently knowledgeable to give you direction without the need to engage your guest directly.

- Low- or no-salt diets, no-beef regimens, and special needs of this nature can be accommodated more easily. These preferences are more widespread and may appear on the menu as a matter of course.

In any event, a gracious host or hostess shouldn't make too much of it when a guest refuses to partake of food or drink. You may make a mental note to find out later whether special dietary requirements prevented the guest from enjoying the meal. Next time, you'll be ready. Your thoughtfulness in the future should make a lasting impression.

Subjects of conversation best left untouched

Not all of the conversation at a mealtime meeting will be of a business nature. However, you should not launch into casual conversation in the same way you might if you were visiting with personal friends. Business gatherings have strict parameters, even if the setting mirrors a friendly, social setting.

Consider the positions of those assembled before you broach certain subjects. A junior executive, for example, may not be privy to a senior executive's failing marriage. If you inquire whether a person is comfortable in a new city residence, you may be putting that person in a position of revealing more of his or her private life than he or she would care to, especially to the junior executive.

Good judgment must prevail before you broach a subject in any setting, but you should be especially aware of what you are saying in the business setting. An insensitive comment can be costly. Friends and family are likely to be more forgiving than a business acquaintance you may have unintentionally offended.

How to get favored treatment at a restaurant

Recognition helps to establish everyone's importance. Accordingly, when you enter the establishment where your mealtime meeting will be conducted, and you are welcomed by name by the captain, maitre d' and others, your guests will be impressed. Moreover, these people will play an important role in making the occasion a success.

It's a mistake to think that generous gratuities alone will win you favored treatment at the places you frequent with business guests. After all, other astute businesspeople provide rewards, too.

Your genuine interest and polite conversation with the people who serve you make a special statement and go a long way toward earning you favored treatment. A verbalized "Thank you" for service at the end of an occasion and compliments extended to the chef, when appropriate, demonstrate your appreciation. When you treat people who take care of your needs kindly, you may expect kind treatment in return.

Four rules that protect a wine novice

For some, the ability to choose the correct wine for the table is a skill that is greatly admired. In any event, no one wishes to appear unworldly when left with the task of choosing the wine for a mealtime meeting.

Here are four pointers that may come to an executive's rescue:

1. A wine steward will be happy to help you make a selection. Ask your waiter to send the wine steward to your table. Rely on his or her advice.

2. When the wine is brought for your approval, don't attempt to examine the cork or fake a ritual you may have observed others engage in. Read the label to confirm that it is the wine you ordered. Sip the wine to make sure it has a pleasing taste. Stop there.

3. If there is a wine expert in your group, you might graciously defer to him or her. You can say, "Sam is our resident wine expert. Sam, would you honor us by making a selection." Not only should Sam be flattered, but your compliment to Sam adds to your gracious manner. In addition, the wine selected should be the right choice.

4. If you must choose on your own, study the wine list for a few moments. Listen to whether the orders include both red meat and fowl. If so, order both red and white wine. If no red meat is ordered, order only white wine. Although not all experts agree, it's unlikely anyone would find this procedure objectionable under the circumstances. In addition, it is not rude to ask if your guests have a preference. Some people are allergic to red wine, for example.

When you are someone else's guest

It's easier to be a considerate guest when you remember the efforts you, or any good host or hostess, must extend to bring an occasion to a successful conclusion. Be the kind of guest you'd like to host.

When others stop at your table

When someone you know approaches the table and you are not the host or hostess, you should not invite the individual to join the group. However, it is proper to make introductions. If the individual is inclined to linger, you can politely dismiss him or her with a comment, such as, "It was nice to see you, Bob. I'll phone you tomorrow so we can talk further."

Can you bring your notebook or calculator to the table?

You should not whip out your notebook, calculator or business papers during the serving of the meal. However, if any of these tools are necessary to facilitate the completion of business, you may announce your intention as you reach for your briefcase, "Jane, I hope you don't mind if I make a few notes. I want to be certain to include all the points you've outlined when we draw up the contract."

If Jane is uncomfortable about your intention, don't carry through with it.

If you use a small calculator or notepad at the table, try to be brief. Put these tools away as soon as you've finished with them. Be as unobtrusive as possible.

Tableside grooming

Personal grooming should not be attended to at the table. If the wind has wreaked havoc with your hair, or your lips feel unusually dry, don't even be tempted to reach for your comb, lip balm, or other grooming aids at the table. Either attend to your grooming needs before going to the table, excuse yourself from the table, or resign yourself to having wind-tossed hair or dry lips.

Some women are in the habit of pulling out a small mirror at the end of the meal in order to perform a quick makeup repair. Even if a touchup takes only a few minutes, tableside grooming is inappropriate. It may take five minutes to walk to the powder room and five minutes to return, but it is better to waste a little time than engage in tableside grooming, which is not at all consistent with good manners.

Maintaining different dietary practices

How do you avoid offending a business host or hostess when he or she makes reservations to meet you for lunch at a famous steak house and you don't eat red meat?

When you have dietary practices that fall outside the norm, there are times when your limitations demand some extra planning. Protecting a well-meaning host or hostess from feeling hurt is one of those times.

- If it is possible to phone a restaurant in advance and inquire if the menu includes foods that will make it easy for you to order, take the time to do so.

- If you learn that the restaurant's menu excludes your personal requirements, you have two choices. Depending upon your relationship with your host or hostess, explain the situation to him or her before the meeting. For example, "Justine, I know the fine reputation Superior Steak House enjoys, but frankly, I don't eat red meat. Can we meet somewhere else?" Or, go to the steak house, order a salad or an omelet, and offer no explanation unless you are asked. You might feel self-conscious carrying out this strategy. But there is a good chance no one will notice or care. Many people these days eat light lunches and it should not be an issue.

3

Reacting to Formal Invitations from Superiors, Associates, Subordinates, Customers and Suppliers

According to the experts, there is established protocol for dealing with invitations to social events that stem from business acquaintances. These social/business invitations are usually extra sensitive in nature, since an individual's invitation is often at the behest of one person who is making arrangements for the event with additional people, who may be concerned about who is invited and who ultimately attends. By its nature, an invitation takes you into another person's personal life and should not be taken lightly.

Your timing and correctness in responding to invitations, no matter who they come from, should always be the same. Obviously, you might go to greater lengths to attend your superior's dinner party or an important customer's affair, in contrast to a subordinate's or supplier's barbecue. There is nothing wrong with different reactions to different invitations as long as you keep them to yourself. But your private thinking and decisions should never be allowed to spill over into the way you respond to invitations. Conveying that you treat any invitation lightly is not only improper, but can lead to business problems. By responding to invitations quickly and politely, you will earn the reputation of being proper and dependable.

How to determine if you are expected to attend

If you receive an invitation from someone, you are expected to attend. In fact, your attendance at a colleague's event can be thought of as a request for your help. You may be considered by your host to be the right person to be charming and engage shy people in conversation. Depending on your position, you may be someone your host or hostess wants to show off. In any case, when you receive an invitation to a social or business function, it is correct to assume that you are expected to attend.

The proper response to invitations

When you receive a formal invitation, or an invitation with an R.S.V.P., you should respond within twenty-four hours, if possible, and definitely within three days. The response should be on formal stationery and handwritten (unless, of course, the R.S.V.P. includes a telephone number for your convenience). Use a stamp on the envelope rather than a postal meter imprint, which is business oriented. The content of your letter should include wording from the invitation and state clearly whether you will or will not attend. You should also give the full name of the person attending with you, and his or her relationship to you (husband, wife, friend, associate), if your invitation includes an unnamed guest.

Here is an example of a response to a formal invitation. It should follow the form of the invitation line for line and be handwritten on white or off-white formal stationery:

Mr. and Mrs. John J. Jones
accept with pleasure
Mr. and Mrs. Thomas Smith's
kind invitation for
Saturday, the twelfth of September
at six o'clock

You should respond to an informal invitation if a response is requested, or if it is an invitation for brunch, lunch or dinner. The response should be made as soon as possible to allow time for arrangements if you can't attend. Your response should follow the tone (dignified, casual) of the invitation. It's wise to repeat the date, time and place to be sure there is no misunderstanding.

An invitation that is made orally, either in person or via the telephone, should be responded to orally. It is proper to ask for time to determine if your schedule is clear. It would, however, be improper to delay a response for more than twenty-four hours. Response can be made by telephone or in person. If a couple is invited by another couple, either spouse can make an acceptance call to either spouse. Repeat date, time and place when accepting an invitation.

The proper way to turn down an invitation

Regrets should be attended to with the same speed as acceptances. Here is an example of how to send regrets when answering a formal invitation. Regrets should also be handwritten on formal paper:

Mr. and Mrs. John J. Jones
regret exceedingly
that a previous engagement
prevents their accepting
Mr. and Mrs. Thomas Smith's
kind invitation for
Saturday, the twelfth of September

An informal invitation can be declined on note paper in your handwriting. It is not considered proper to give a long account of why you cannot attend. Here is an example of how to send regrets to an informal invitation:

25

Dear Jim & Carol:

Frank and I have a previous engagement on September 12th and are sorry that we will not be able to attend your cocktail party. We look forward to seeing you in the near future.

The same tone and contents used for an informal invitation can be used to decline an oral invitation, in person or via the telephone.

Should you send a gift even if you don't attend?

If the event is centered upon a third party, such as a wedding to which you're invited by the parents, a gift is definitely in order. The gift's value should be no less than the gift you would have given had you attended. Aside from weddings, this practice applies to confirmations, bar or bas mitzvahs, anniversary and graduation parties, and other events where a person is honored or is the central attraction.

House gifts that are customarily given when attending dinner parties and similar occasions are not required when you do not attend. It is considered thoughtful, however, if you send flowers or a bottle or two of fine wine to the house in which the dinner party will take place. The gift should arrive on the day of the dinner party or the day before. The note accompanying the flowers or wine should not refer to your lack of attendance. It can simply be signed or you can include a few words such as, "We hope you and your dinner guests have a wonderful time."

4

Business Gift-Giving That's in Good Taste

Adhering to accepted protocol when giving business gifts can help to avoid embarrassment and the appearance of unintended questionable business practices. In some companies, the acceptance of business gifts is strictly prohibited. Under such circumstances, employees of the company and its suppliers are clearly informed of this policy. Yet gift-giving is a business custom that is considered appropriate by most people so long as this practice is carried out in good taste.

There are times when presenting a gift is inappropriate, and times when the presentation of a gift may be poorly timed. The kind of gift, its value, how it is presented, and other factors often determine its acceptability. Avoiding the practice of gift-giving can work against you due to tradition. Some people expect gifts. Others believe they deserve them. By not presenting gifts you can hurt your business. On the other hand, the presentation of gifts can also hurt business and has even been known to ruin careers.

The following questions and answers will shed light on the when, how and what of gift-giving that is in good taste:

Q. When is a gift in order?

A. A gift should be given to signify a business friendship and to acknowledge appreciation of a business acquaintance who has been thoughtful of you. A gift should never be given as a direct response to the receipt of an order, purchase, or the like. Gifts are also in order to business colleagues' spouses or children to acknowledge major events for which gift-giving is customary (weddings, anniversaries, etc.).

Q. What if a company's policy disallows acceptance of gifts?

A. In this case, gifts should not be given. If there is a dollar limit on a gift's value, adhere to it. Doing otherwise is not only poor protocol but can also jeopardize your relationship with an individual, place him or her in an uncomfortable position, or cause the person's company to take serious action against the individual. If it is permissible, instead of presenting a gift, you might invite the person involved and his or her spouse to be your guest at the theatre or dinner. But make certain this is not at odds with company policy. At the least, a personal note to the person can make your appreciation known. Do not mention that you would have preferred sending a gift had it been allowed.

Q. Would it be correct to send a gift to a customer's spouse or child if company policy precludes presenting gifts?

A. No. It is considered proper to follow a company's policy by observing its spirit and avoiding any loopholes in the wording of its policy.

Q. What would constitute a proper gift?

A. According to Letitia Baldrige, world-renowned expert on etiquette, a gift should be creative, and something you know the recipient will enjoy.

Q. What about the value of a gift?

A. The value should not be high or low. A gift that costs about $25 would be considered proper. A gift from one chief executive to another might cost somewhere between $50 and $100.

Q. Where should the gift be delivered?

A. Ideally, the gift should be delivered to the individual's home. Liquor or wine should always be sent to the home.

Q. Should a note accompany the gift?

A. Yes. But the note's contents should never refer to business or thank the recipient for business.

Q. Should I expect a gift in return?

A. No. The proper response, in most cases, would be a thank-you note acknowledging your gift.

Q. Are there any laws relative to gift-giving?

A. Yes. First, the tax rules limit deductions for business gifts to $25 per gift. Second, a federal anti-bribery law prohibits gift-giving by customers to officials of financial institutions. While the law is worded so as to prohibit virtually any gift one could think of, it is being interpreted by many to mean gifts of money or those worth more than $50. Some financial institutions have adopted conflict-of-interest guidelines that disallow the acceptance of gifts of any kind, no matter how small their value. There are penalties for the customer gift-giver and financial institution official gift-receiver if found in violation of this law. Obviously, this goes well beyond company policy. Even if you have been giving a gift to your banker for years, it would be best to check with him or her first, before presenting a gift under this relatively new set of circumstances.

Q. Is it proper to give a gift in person?

A. Yes, if the gift is small enough for the recipient to handle. A special visit to a person's home to deliver a business gift is not considered proper, unless you are an invited guest and the gift is directly related to the event you are attending.

Q. Are personal types of gifts in order?

A. Business gifts should not be of a personal nature. Such items as clothing should be avoided. An exception to this rule might be a wallet or a handbag.

Selecting the proper gift

The key to having someone truly appreciate and enjoy a gift you present is selecting the right gift for a specific person. This is far more important than the gift's extrinsic value. Such a gift is appreciated since it's something the recipient would obviously enjoy. Also, it conveys a sense that you gave the gift some thought and didn't run out and buy three dozen of the same item to hand out because you felt obligated to give gifts.

Often, if you know the person for whom you're buying a gift, you are aware of his or her hobbies and interests. There are many items available, including books, gadgets, magazine subscriptions and other selections related to a hobby or interest. Potential gifts cover a wide range of merchandise and gift-givers often select quality items even in low price ranges. They look for the kind of gift people may have always wanted, but tend not to buy for themselves. For example, a fine bookmark that costs $25 is a little luxury that might be appreciated.

These kinds of gifts include:

- A silver or gold pen.
- An appointment book or desk diary.
- Engraved gold or silver items, such as key rings.
- For smokers: Cigarette, cigar or pipe lighters.
- For fishing buffs: Tackle boxes filled with tackle.
- For tennis players: A pressurized ball container.
- For bicycling enthusiasts: An odometer.
- For joggers: A timepiece or special runner's key holder.
- For golfers: Personalized golf balls.
- For boaters: A gadget or plaque for the boat.
- For skiers: Goggles.

Or, there are other selections:

- Cuff links or a small pin.

- A small piece of crystal for the desk or home.
- A basket of gourmet foods, or exotic teas and coffees.
- A couple of bottles of fine wine or a bottle of a favorite liquor.

Use these suggestions to set off your own creative juices. Some gifts are safer to give than others. Unless you are certain that a person will appreciate a more specialized kind of gift, it is best to stay with a more general kind of gift that is not intended for a particular activity. If you know a person has certain interests, but you're not sure if he or she already owns what you have in mind, you can purchase a gift certificate from a store that stocks that particular kind of merchandise. Since many people feel a gift certificate comes close to giving cash, use care in making that selection. Finally, if you have any doubts as to whether someone would appreciate or be comfortable with a certain gift, make a different selection. It's wiser to play it safe. Flowers or a plant are always appropriate.

5

When You Receive
Business Gifts

When you receive a gift you have a bit less control of things. Obviously, the gift-giver must initiate things. You cannot stop the act of giving. Since you cannot make a judgment over a package you receive until you have opened it, the choice of receiving gifts is really not within your control. It is your judgment whether or not to accept a gift that counts.

There are proper ways to refuse gifts and methods of refusal that comply with virtually every company's set of policies on gifts. Among other things, you would probably prefer not to make waves for the person who, with good intentions, presents you with a gift you can't keep. On the other hand, it would be imprudent for you not to take some action that documents your compliance with proper business practices and company policy.

In cases where a gift is appropriate and you accept it, the way to acknowledge it graciously is covered for you in Chapter 6, *Letter-Writing Skills That Convey a Sense of Business Etiquette*.

Note: If you are an official of a financial institution, check to see that your firm's policy reflects the federal law which regulates receipt of gifts.

How to determine if a gift is appropriate

The main point to consider when deciding whether it is appropriate to accept a business gift is its appearance to others. Even if you are positive that a gift presented to you is clearly not a bribe nor represents in any other way a conflict of interest, it must pass the appearance test. If it could reasonably appear that the gift represents something more than a traditional acknowledgment from one business colleague to another, it should not be accepted. Here are some questions to help you come to a decision:

- Is the value of the gift excessive?
- Was the gift presented at some time other than traditional and customary gift-giving times?
- Would your acceptance of the gift violate company policy?
- Might you feel obligated to the party presenting the gift?
- Have you concluded a business contract or other activity in the last three months or so to the advantage of the gift-giver?
- Does the gift-giver have a reputation for "buying" people?

If you answer yes to any of these questions, more than likely the gift should be declined. It is better to err in favor of declining the gift over accepting it and taking a chance on being hurt by it at some future date.

When your verdict is to decline the gift

As stated earlier, you do not have control over someone else's actions. It's not in your power to prevent someone from presenting a gift to you. Opening a package delivered by mail or courier, of which you have no prior knowledge, does not necessarily constitute acceptance of its contents. Once you are aware of the gift, however, lack of action can be construed as an official acceptance. Following are recommendations you can use when refusing a gift:

- Take action immediately, or certainly within twenty-four hours.
- The gift should be returned with a note that thanks the gift-giver but makes it clear that the gift cannot be accepted. (Sample notes can be found near the end of this chapter.)
- Keep a copy of the note for your own protection.
- Reporting the receipt and return of the gift to superiors and others is in order only if this is a company requirement, or you know for sure that the gift was intended as a bribe.

The proper way to refuse a gift

Within the time frame set forth above, compose a "thank-you, but no-thank-you" note that is dated and states when you received the gift and that it is enclosed and refused. The note should not convey a negative tone. It is not proper to scold the gift-giver, be insulting, or indicate anger. The note should be in your handwriting. Here are two examples you can adapt:

If the gift is against your company's policy, it's best to cite the policy as an excuse for the refusal—

(Date)

Dear Jane/Jim:

Thank you for the (description of gift) you were thoughtful enough to send to me on (date received).

Although I sincerely appreciate your sentiments, company policy precludes my acceptance of the gift, which is enclosed with this note.

Sincerely,
(signed)

If the refusal is based solely on your own determination—

(Date)

Dear Jane/Jim:

Thank you for the (description of gift) you were thoughtful enough to send me on (date received).

Although I sincerely appreciate your sentiments, the gift is not appropriate for me to keep and is enclosed with this note.

Sincerely,
(signed)

There is no need to call the gift-giver in advance of refusal. The gift should not be brought up in conversation. If the gift-giver mentions your refusal in conversation, you can either move on to another topic or repeat what you said in your note. Should the gift-giver contact you after receiving the returned gift, graciously accept an apology if one is offered, or politely repeat what is in your note if there is further mention of the gift.

6

Letter-Writing Skills
That Convey
a Sense
of Business Etiquette

A business letter conveys more than words you set to paper. If you are late in sending a letter, no matter what you say in it, it will carry the connotation that you consider other matters more important or, worse yet, that the person (not the letter) slipped your mind.

Phrases used in a letter often make the writer seem pompous when this is not intended. Many executives who write business letters use loftier tones and words than they do when they talk to someone. This can give the recipient of the letter the wrong idea. And sometimes writers of business letters get caught up in purple prose and ramble on without saying what they mean to. Finally, the way a letter looks conveys a great deal. The paper stock, letterhead, salutation, margins, spelling accuracy, and lack of correction marks all play a major role in setting the right image and making the correct statement.

At times a specific kind of letter is in order and its absence is quite naturally conspicuous. In our culture, one who overlooks business etiquette rarely, if ever, has it called to his or her attention. It's important, therefore, to make certain that an image does not suffer due to the neglect of what is considered the "veneer" of younger executives and the sense of duty of seasoned executives. A simple thank-you letter can often leave a lasting impression with a major customer or client. Moreover, an expected letter that is overlooked can sour a budding business relationship.

The correct letter, written and presented properly, is neither difficult nor time-consuming to execute. There are several points of etiquette to keep in mind when a letter is expected of you.

Keep it short and to the point

A famous writer once opened a letter to a friend by stating, "Please excuse this long letter. I did not have the time to write a short one." Keeping a letter short does take a little extra effort. But it demonstrates your regard for the recipient's time. A shorter letter is also usually more to the point and easier to understand. Shortness should not be measured by the number of pages, but by saying what you want to say with the fewest words possible. You can accomplish this by using the following methods, which will become easier after the first few letters:

- Write or dictate your letter as if the person to whom it's addressed is sitting across the desk from you.

- If you're not dictating, talk out loud as you write. This will help you to use the expressions and words you normally use when you are at ease.

- To start off easily, determine what you want to say before you compose your letter. Then say it, even if it doesn't seem to be coming out exactly right.

- Once the draft is typed, read it through from beginning to end without making judgments. Then, reread it and check for any words that can be deleted without altering the meaning.

- Take a hard look at your first two paragraphs. Non-professional writers generally do not convey important points in their opening paragraphs. If this is the case with your letter, see if sentences can be combined and simplified. In some instances, you might find that you can delete the first one or two paragraphs without missing them.

- Check to see if you are saying the same thing more than once. If so, delete repetitions.
- Read the letter once more to determine if you are conveying what you intend to. If you have any doubts about a word or sentence, assume that your doubts are correct and make the necessary changes.
- Before you sign the letter make certain it looks right. How does it "sit" on the page? Are the margins wide enough? Are there correction marks? Has the letter been proofread? Did someone double-check spelling, especially of names?

When is a letter in order?

There are times when the omission of a letter is considered rude, and other times when it is not mandatory, but makes good business sense:

- A note is in order when someone gives you a gift.
- A written response is called for when you receive a written invitation.
- A bread-and-butter note is a must after staying in a person's home for a weekend or longer. Sending flowers with the note is not considered overdoing it.
- It is considered thoughtful and gracious, but not strictly necessary, to write a thank-you note for a dinner or cocktail party.
- When an associate or colleague is promoted, a congratulatory note is appropriate.
- A note is a nice gesture when any business person with whom you come in contact is married, celebrates the birth of a child, receives an honor, and so forth.

- A condolence note should be written if you were a friend or associate of either the deceased or a surviving relative.

When should you simply pen a note?

Handwritten notes are preferred when sending notes or letters of congratulation, appreciation, thanks, apology (to cancel an appointment) and condolence. Informal invitations should also be handwritten.

A letter of introduction is proper only if, in your view, both people will benefit from it. If you hand it to the bearer, the letter should be unsealed. Using a calling card alone, without a letter, is not considered to be in good taste.

When family or personal references are appropriate

Generally it is not advisable to refer to family members or make personal references unless you have met the person to whom you are referring and know for sure that the person is currently associated with the individual to whom you're writing. For example:

- If you have not been in touch with a person for years and have reason to write, it is best not to refer to the person's spouse unless you are certain they are still married.
- Reference to people or happenings should not be based on hearsay. If someone tells you Bill is buying a new home, do not refer to it unless Bill has told you about it. Should you hear that Bill's wife is ill, avoid mention of it unless Bill has mentioned it to you.
- If you have met an individual's spouse or child, it is proper to send your regards to them. If you were made aware of a personal project the person to

whom you're writing has undertaken, it is in good taste to ask how it's coming along.

Sample letters you can use

The following sample letters can be used as guides to save time when composing your own letters:

... A letter of congratulations. (*Handwritten*)

Dear George:
So glad to hear about your promotion....
It's always a pleasure to hear good news about someone you know and admire.
Congratulations and best wishes.

Sincerely,
(signed)

Dear Fred:
Congratulations on (your birthday, the birth of your child, your anniversary, etc.).
It's always a pleasure to write about happy events in the lives of (friends, associates, colleagues, etc.).
Best wishes.

Sincerely,
(signed)

... A letter of appreciation. *(Handwritten)*

Note: A bread-and-butter note should be addressed to the hostess, unless the host lives alone. This holds true even if the host invited you. Mail it two or three days after leaving.

Dear Mary:
I want you to know how much I appreciated your fine hospitality during my visit to your home.
The cocktail party on Saturday was a delight and

I enjoyed meeting Bob and Janice. Indeed, you are lucky to have them as close friends.

Thank you so much for a wonderful three days.

Sincerely,
(signed)

... Thank-you letter for a gift. (*Handwritten*)

Note: Letter should be sent within a week of receipt.

Dear Herb and Janet:

Thank you for your thoughtfulness in selecting the beautiful vase as a gift for our sixth wedding anniversary.

The decorative design on the vase matches perfectly with the decor in our dining room. We have already placed it on the middle shelf of our china closet.

Sincerely,
(signed)

... Letter of condolence. (*Handwritten on formal paper*)

Note: Try to compose a note that states what you would say if you met the bereaved in person. If you knew the deceased, mention a quality; otherwise, reflect on the fine reputation of the deceased.

Dear Sally:

I want you to know how sorry I was to learn of the death of your....

It was my pleasure to work side by side with your ... for twelve years. He/she was always ready to lend a helping hand anytime one of his/her co-workers had a problem. Indeed, he/she will be missed by all who had the good fortune to know him/her.

His/her wonderful ways will last in my memory

forever. If I can be of help to you during this difficult time, please let me know.

Sincerely,
(signed)

...Letter of introduction.

Note: A letter of introduction requests the extension of hospitality from one person to another at your request.

Dear Michael:
  I would like to introduce you to Gary Jones, who has just relocated to San Francisco and probably could make good use of your experience as a twenty-year resident of the city.
  Gary shares your interest in photography and has a great deal of experience in wildlife "shooting."
  Any help you can give to Gary would be appreciated.

Sincerely,
(signed)

...Letter of apology. (*Handwritten*)

Dear Edgar:
  Please accept my sincere apology for having to cancel our luncheon last Wednesday on short notice.
  About two hours before we were to meet, I was informed by my home-town police that my house had been burglarized. I had to get over to my house immediately and get a locksmith to install new locks.
  If you want to hear the rest of the story and find out how things turned out, you will have to be my guest for lunch. I will call you next week.
  Sorry about the inconvenience I caused.

Sincerely,
(signed)

7

Telephone Manners
That Say More
Than Any Conversation

"It ain't what you say, it's the way that you say it" is a phrase borrowed from an old song that helps to spotlight a vital communication technique that can work for or against you every time you pick up the telephone during the business day.

According to Laura Darius, president of Corporate Communication Skills, Inc., a training and consulting firm serving New York-based clients, voice skills usually need improvement. "Highly placed executives usually have a good deal of facility on the phone, with the exception of voice. Sometimes there may be voice problems; occasionally some diction needs work."

Darius, working on a project for the Bermuda Office of Tourism, says voice and pacing skills, as well as good manners, are the skills that count. "When someone calls the tour office and speaks with a representative who has a gruff or disinterested response and doesn't present a positive image, the feeling is that the caller is likely to contact [the competition]."

Steps that can improve how employees say it

There are ways to help an employee improve telephone clarity and present a positive telephone image. Here are some pointers you can give:

- *Don't mumble*. Focus on the reason for the call. If necessary, plan the opening line. Try not to be distracted by papers on your desk or other matters during the course of a phone conversation.

- *Speak slowly.* Rapid speech may result in sounds and syllables that can't be understood by the listener. Remember, in-person conversation gives the listener the advantage of watching what is being said along with hearing what is said. When the listener must rely on hearing only, every sound helps.

- *Use vocal variety.* If employees are enthusiastic about what they are saying, their pitches will automatically rise on adjectives. Their rhythm will be livelier. If not in a positive frame of mind, they should postpone initiating important business calls.

- *Let the voice project energy.* This may be easier if one imagines talking to a person face to face. If an employee has to spend a lot of time on the phone, it's good to get up out of the chair occasionally while talking. "Dancing with the receiver" may improve delivery.

- *Smile from time to time.* The pleasantness of the smile is usually transmitted to the person on the other end of the line. Courteous phrases, such as, "Thanks so much for your time" or, "Good of you to return my call so promptly," help to send a smile over the line, too.

- *The mouthpiece should be about one inch from the lips.* If employees cradle the receiver against their necks, many of their words will bounce off to the side. If they must take notes or keep their hands free when talking on the telephone, consider getting them a headset or some other telephone instrument(s) so that delivery to the transmitter isn't compromised.

- *Keep a heavy accent in check.* The person should slow down his or her speech pattern. The listener will probably need an extra beat to absorb the employee's pronunciation. You may want to keep this in mind if you travel to distant locations on business. A successful telephone pace on your home turf may need to be slowed down when you are away, or calling long distance.

- *No gum drops, please.* If employees smoke, drink, suck on candies or clutter their mouths in any way while on the telephone, their listeners may pick up sounds that suggest they're otherwise occupied. Loud chewing or sipping noises are nothing short of rude. Pauses and noises that accompany a "drag" on a cigarette can also be irritating.

When you know how to say it

The most skillful telephone user is probably using the telephone as a selling tool. Insurance salespeople or registered representatives, for example, work to sharpen their skills almost every business day. Seminars, specialized training programs and endless practice sessions enable them to hone their telephone skills. These talents go far beyond knowing how to say it.

Admittedly, there's a good deal to know about the most constructive ways to use the telephone:

- *The times your secretary shouldn't place the call for you:*
  —Any time you have to cancel an appointment that is imminent.

    If, for example, an executive has a lunch date with a client in one hour but there's an equipment breakdown at the plant and the executive must deal with the problem immediately, he or she should take a moment to call the client first. If that is not possible, get another executive to call with apologies. A call from a secretary appears to be more routine than your direct call or a call from another executive.

—When you are calling a direct number and it's likely that the party you wish to speak with will pick up the telephone.

—When you aren't ready.

It's inconsiderate to initiate a call and then make the individual wait for you.

You don't want to waste time with the in-between people who normally handle the phone for the individual you want to speak with, so you instruct your secretary to "please get Harry Insulated on the line." But while waiting, you start to add some figures and don't pick up your phone when your secretary signals. Harry Insulated has every reason to feel slightly annoyed by this inconsiderate treatment.

• *When you have to return a call, be prompt.*

Your earliest attention to a promise or request that you call back is, in itself, a courteous response. If you have bad news to report or pass along you will lighten the load by being courteous and prompt. "Sue, I'm afraid I have some bad news. The powers that be decided to award the contract to another supplier." Sue may be disappointed, but she will appreciate your prompt response.

If you hesitate to return a call because you don't have enough background information, or don't know the person who called, don't feel obligated to respond. If the message-taker was negligent in getting more information, it's a good time to remind that individual to flesh out information from callers in the future.

• *When you don't want to accept a call*, it's best to make it clear at the outset that you do not wish to speak to the caller.

Do not avoid the caller by asking your secretary or assistant to say that you're not in, and don't give an excuse like, "I'm busy now, can you call at another time?" Eventually, the caller will realize he or she is getting the runaround, and a runaround is a rude maneuver. Therefore, use this approach: "Mr. Brown advises all suppliers to contact appropriate department heads. He never accepts calls himself. I can direct you to the right person, if you care to give me more information. And, it's probably better for you to write to that person rather than call."

- *When you sense that someone does not want to talk with you*, be quick to stress a benefit.

"Bob Helpful suggested that I call. Our new payroll program saves small retailers three days each month in record-keeping chores. Would you have a moment to talk now, or would you prefer that I call back?" If the listener agrees to talk now, he or she has agreed to continue the conversation and is likely to relax and listen. If the person says he or she is too busy, it may be so. It's discourteous to force yourself on someone who is otherwise engaged. When you call back, you can honestly say, "Jane Smith asked me to call." In any event, you have taken steps to diffuse the negative response and set the stage for conversation.

- *An important caller may be discourteous.*

He or she talks to others while talking to you on the telephone. For example, a client calls, "Charley, it's time we did something about this ABC report you worked up for me. Sally, get me that file. Dave, cancel that order. Oh, yes, Charley, why don't you handle job bid requests for us?" Must you continue the conversation under these circumstances? Sometimes you must. But not always. Suggest in-person meetings and keep telephone business down to a minimum. Or, you may ask him or her to repeat what has been said, pleading, "Mr. Jones, it's difficult to hear you, we probably have a poor connection." When you originate calls to this individual you can say, "Mr. Jones, I need your undivided attention. I promise, I'll be as brief as possible." Once in a while, you might get his undivided attention.

When you must cut a telephone conversation short

There are times when executives must end telephone conversations but the party on the line makes it difficult. This can be handled with finesse:

- *Some callers simply don't get to the point.* If they ramble, you can politely request, "Ms. Linger, what exactly is it you have in mind?" If the direct approach doesn't help, you can say, "Ms. Linger, I have to prepare for a meeting. I don't have much time; what would you suggest?"

- *Some callers race on without giving you a chance to speak.* In that instance you have little choice but to talk over them. "Excuse me, Mr. Fast, I don't think it's me you want to speak to. Sounds like a problem for our sales representative. I'll switch the call, please hold." Occasionally, a caller is forced to talk quickly to avoid being switched from place to place without anyone understanding what he or she wants. So, if you do cut a caller short by transferring the call, try not to perpetuate the dilemma.

- *You run into a chummy caller you don't know.* "Hello, Carol, a friend of yours told me to call." The person is evasive except for repeated use of your first name. Direct him or her to make a specific request. "It's best if you put your proposal in writing. Do you have my business address?" Then you can end the conversation by saying, "I'll be waiting for the material to arrive." Now hang up. Courtesy demands that if you get a written communication from this individual, you respond. On the chance that this caller was directed to call you by a friend, you haven't dismissed him or her abruptly. Sometimes, callers who don't know you and want to make a request are nervous, not insincere. On the other hand, someone who isn't sincere is not likely to contact you by letter as well as by phone.

• *Take charge with a caller who has something important to say, but is repetitive.* "George, everything you've said has been helpful. Let me give you a quick summary of the high points.... We'll speak again at the end of the week." Don't allow yourself to be diverted. Deliver the summary. Say "Thank you" and "Good-bye."

• *There's a knack for handling a rude caller.* First, try to "kill him with kindness." Of course, you can always hang up, but in the business setting this isn't advisable, since you do not act strictly for yourself but as a company representative. Unless the caller gets abusive, try allowing him or her to let off steam. "Mr. Casey, I understand your anger. That shipment should have been delivered by now. I'll check into it immediately and call you within the hour." You can hang up. By the time you return the call, Mr. Casey should have cooled off. Of course, you should be true to your word and return the call within the hour. Even if you can only report that you're still investigating, Mr. Casey will know that you are looking after his needs.

• *Any time you are stuck, enlist the aid of your secretary or assistant.* Some experts advise setting up a signal so your secretary will ring you on another line, with the sound loud enough to be heard by your caller. Or, your assistant can enter the room and loudly announce that you have a long-distance call waiting. Numerous preplanned ploys may be used to enable you to cut away. Others rely on a fictitious interruption. "Sally, my secretary has just signaled me that I must take another call. Let's talk again soon."

- *Finally*, some busy people start most conversations with a warning. "Marge, it's hectic here today. Let's talk fast." The stage is immediately set for keeping the telephone conversation short.

8

Setting the Stage for More Genteel Customer Service

When it comes to customer relations, it's up to the company employees, from the Chief Executive Officer to mailroom clerks, to put their best foot forward on behalf of the company.

Good business etiquette, proper manners and respect for the customer are vital to business success.

When any form of communication is weakened, the company is vulnerable to loss of customer goodwill and eventual loss of profits.

Considering the dollars expended to advertise and promote products or services, it makes sense to strengthen the lines of communication so that customers are kept happy, and the relationship between company and customer is a long and profitable one.

No matter what your product or service, or what type of business you are in, there are essentially three lines of communication open between your company and each customer. They are: Correspondence, Telephone and Face-to-Face Encounter.

Corresponding with customers

Many organizations mail predesigned letters or forms to customers or clients that serve a number of purposes. No matter what purpose is served when sending correspondence, two questions should be asked:

1. How does it look?
2. How does it sound?

Written communication that is difficult to read because the print is too light or blurred doesn't make a good appearance. As a result, the content of the communication is at a disadvantage from the outset.

Other factors that contribute to the look of correspondence are:

- *Size of type.* It may be difficult for older customers to read fine print. If your market is comprised of many older people, simply enlarging the print could improve customer communications.

- *Layout.* Is there room on the form for a person to fill in the information you request? If the message has personalized information added to a printed form, does it show up clearly, or does it fall in a haphazard manner, making it difficult to read?

- *Handwritten messages* tend to lend a more friendly look to the communication. Preprinted forms that are used to extend an apology can seem friendlier if they include a handwritten sentence or two.

The tone of the message says something about the way the company feels about its customers.

- *Polite requests* sound different from requests phrased as demands. The word "please" can make the difference. For example, "Please fill in all spaces," rather than "Fill in all spaces."

- *Closing.* Does your closing simply say, "Customer Service Department," or does it include a person's name? A vague catch-all like a department title is extremely impersonal. If possible, the name of a person who is there and can be contacted by the customer should appear at the end of the communication. Many forms have a space for a signature but do not contain one. The empty space detracts from the importance of the communication.

Note: Correspondence that has been planned and written by experts may contain all the courteous elements. But the good intentions are lost when fill-in spaces and signatures are left blank.

Telephone service

Everyone has had occasion to be frustrated when making business calls. The list of abuses is long: the abrupt way a telephone is answered, the length of time it takes to reach the correct individual, long periods of unsolicited music assaulting your ears while you hold, and being disconnected before you've completed your business.

When one firm in an industry tightens up its customer relations more than others (competitors), the weaker customer relations practices become conspicuous. And in some industries, such as banking and travel, the only thing that really separates firms, with the exception of a few pricing differences, is the quality of service. "It's just amazing," a customer service training consultant says, "the number of people who are not shopping someplace because of the way they were treated."

He suggests "a mystery shopper service" as a method to show a client how telephone business is conducted at his or her firm.

The following are actual comments from shopper reports:

Employee: "To be perfectly honest with you, I'm sure you could get a better deal somewhere else."

Shopper: "Exactly what do you do in this department?"

Employee: "You know, I work here all day every day, but I'm really not sure what we do here!" or, "We only give that information to preferred customers."

Need more be said?

New Jersey National Bank designed an action center to deal with customer questions, complaints and problems. The twenty people who answer phones at the action center can usually answer questions on the spot. If they have to get additional information, they promise to phone the customer back as soon as possible.

Well-trained staffers at the telephone action center are backed up with a personal computer at each desk, which enables them to retrieve current information as they assist callers. By the time an employee gets to the action center, he or she has had some 405 hours of classroom work and 450 hours of hands-on experience.

Customer complaints have fallen by 50%, the bank says. And letters that in the past read, "Your inept people couldn't get my problem solved," have generally been replaced with, "Your representative tried to help me, but the problem still hasn't been solved."

It's obvious that delivery of the best possible telephone service requires a blending of many skills. Some important guidelines:

- *Phone voice.* 38% of a message in a face-to-face conversation is revealed by tone of voice, according to an expert's estimate. That percentage increases in a telephone conversation. Voices that sound bored or robotlike undermine the representative's effectiveness. On the other hand, a pleasant voice should influence a caller favorably. Although representatives can learn to improve their phone voices, it is best to consider this attribute when hiring people who will spend concentrated hours working on the telephone.

- *Taking time to listen.* Customer-contact representatives have to be good listeners. If a representative doesn't listen carefully, he or she may misdirect a caller. Aside from agitating the caller, more time will then be needed to route the caller to the correct party. That time could otherwise be spent servicing another caller.

- *Accurate messages.* When a company representative takes an order and doesn't accurately record information such as size, color and quantity, a good deal of time and money will be wasted. The customer may even decide to cancel the order and purchase the merchandise from a competitor.

- *Delivering messages*. The most accurate message won't be of any value if it isn't delivered. If a secretary isn't prompt about telling the boss that an important client called and wants to be called back as soon as possible, the client won't receive the deserved prompt response. It may be helpful if the executive who is away remembers to ask for phone messages as soon as he or she returns to the office.

- *Transferring calls*. The clicks and noise that spill into the caller's ear when a call is transferred may be difficult to avoid. However, if the caller is properly informed that the call will be transferred and it is necessary to put the line on hold, he or she should appreciate the considerate manner in which the transfer is made. It's a good idea to furnish the caller with the name and extension number of the party to whom the call is being transferred. Then, should the caller be disconnected, he or she will not have to begin all over again to locate the appropriate individual.

- *Answering the phone promptly*. Although experts differ slightly, most suggest answering the telephone on the first or second ring. When a client or customer has to wait for ten or more rings before the telephone is answered, he or she is likely to feel ignored. This is certainly a breach of business etiquette.

- *Explaining delays*. If you must leave the caller to check on records, say so. "Mr. Smith, I'll have to check our files, I hope you don't mind waiting." When you return to the caller, begin by saying, "Thank you for waiting."

- *Using the customer's name.* Refer to the customer by name during the course of conversation, if you can do so smoothly. "Mrs. Graham, we appreciate your business, thank you for calling." It is important to pronounce the name correctly. If Mrs. Graham announces herself to you as Ms. Graham, you should use that form of address.

- *Be natural* but don't let your professionalism slip by using slang or phrases that are more appropriate for use with friends and personal conversations.

- *When the conversation comes to a close.* End the call with care. "Mr. Steward, I'll put a letter of confirmation in the mail today. Thank you again for your time. Good-bye." An abrupt good-bye is like a curt dismissal. Take care to hang up the phone gently.

What you should know about recorded telephone messages and a score card to rate them

Recorded messages have become a tool for some companies intent upon extending service to callers when the office is closed or unattended. They are also used to answer phones when a representative is unable to do so, but will be able to come on the line in short order.

Although opinions vary on whether or not to use recorded messages, a consensus of opinion emerges on how to make them more acceptable.

If you utilize a recorded message on your home telephone answering machine, at your office, or for the company's incoming customer calls, the same guidelines apply. The checklist that follows will help you evaluate any system:

- *Is your machine activated on the first or second ring?* Place a call to the recorder to determine how long the phone rings before it is answered. If the phone rings more than twice before being answered, the device should be adjusted. (This may not be possible for a large telephone system that handles numerous incoming calls at the same time.) The caller may be taken by surprise when a phone rings more than twice and is then answered by a machine. He or she may begin speaking and feel foolish. Faster response time should help spare your caller this discomfort.

- *Does the message make it clear from the start that the caller has reached a machine?* In some cases this can be accomplished by using a stranger's voice to make the recording. For example, if a female secretary usually answers the phone at the office, a male can make the recorded message for the answering machine. And, if you normally answer your own phone, ask a friend of the opposite sex to record your message. The quicker you alert the caller to the fact that he or she has reached a recording device, the better. The opening sentence is of value, too. "No one is available to answer the phone. Robert James will return your call as soon as possible," offers an early clue that the caller has reached a recorded message.

- *Does the message use short sentences that give information clearly?* Callers who hear a recorded message aren't likely to give their full attention to what they hear. Instead, they ponder, "Shall I hang up?" "What should I say?" They know their response will be recorded, and may feel reluctant to commit their messages to tape. Short sentences that give clear directions or other information don't require much of the caller's concentration. In this way, you're telling the caller, "I really want to hear what you have to tell me."

- *Is space for message-taking too limited?* If there's very little space for the caller to leave a message, he or she will be abruptly disconnected. This is a little like having someone hang up on the caller before business has been concluded. It could be that your callers need more time to complete their communications. If, for example, you travel and can't be reached easily during normal business hours, your callers should be given ample opportunity to express themselves on tape. If you or the person responsible for retrieving recorded phone messages notice that several callers are cut off each week, perhaps you should increase response space.

- *How soon does the caller hear the beep?* Most answering devices ask the caller to start talking after hearing the tone. If the tone doesn't sound almost immediately after the recorded message has concluded, the caller may begin to wonder if he or she has missed hearing it. When you check to hear how your answering machine performs, take note of when the tone sounds. A delayed tone may confuse your caller. It doesn't speak well for the way you greet people who do business with you.

- *Is your message appropriate?* When you leave the office to take a two-week vacation, go out of town for a three-day seminar or are generally unavailable, your message will probably need to be different from usual. It may be accurate when it announces, "Gail Grey will return your call as soon as possible." However, a phone call returned one week later is not what the caller expected. Don't neglect to update your message as needed.

- *Periodic checkups.* It's a good idea to call your own answering machine from time to time. A customer or client might not tell you that a high-pitched noise accompanies your message. An unwelcome addition to your message, such as interference, should be corrected quickly. Without checking personally, you won't necessarily know about a problem that exists and needs corrective measures.

If your company has an answering device on-line until

a representative is free to handle a call, it's a good idea to monitor it, too—and to do so at different times of the day.

Most frustrating to callers is the long delay from the time the caller is greeted to the time a representative is available. In order to give your customers considerate telephone service, it may be necessary to have more representatives handling incoming calls during peak calling hours. If this is not possible, consider whether the recorded answer and long delay alienates your customers. Callers might be served better with a busy signal. If there is usually a sufficient number of representatives answering the telephone, the caller shouldn't continue to be greeted with a busy signal for long.

When an electronic device is used to pick up incoming calls on non-toll-free lines, the customer may have good reason to feel angry. He or she is literally paying for any slow, questionable service.

When you deal with a great number of callers each business day:

- Is the message clear and the voice that delivers it pleasant?
- Does a message come back on the line to reassure the caller while he or she continues to hold?
- Is your typical caller likely to find certain music abrasive?
- Are representatives coming on-line after a reasonable interval?
- Do representatives thank the caller for waiting?

Answers to these questions should lead to one of three conclusions:

—Your company is providing good recorded answering service to callers.

—There's room for improvement.

—You don't have some of the answers. If so, it may be time to call on an expert to help evaluate and strengthen your system.

Face-to-face customer service

Delivery of top-notch face-to-face customer service depends upon a combination of various efforts.

Barbara Aron Cahan, a management training consultant with Associated Seminars, a New Jersey-based company, served as Director of Training and Development for Caesars Atlantic City Hotel Casino. Cahan explains that although most people want to perform well, "they may be preoccupied with personal concerns, home problems, health problems and insecurities about how their employers view their performance." As a result, they tend to be inattentive to customer needs.

According to Cahan, "Training should start at the top. Some executives don't realize that people have to know where they stand." Small incentives such as a verbal pat on the back can be very meaningful to the front-line employee facing the public.

Well-rounded training programs must work to help employees develop a positive mental attitude and cope with stress. And they should teach the basics, like good grooming. When Cahan trains personnel in proper grooming skills, she bills it as a fun course and prefers to have twelve to fifteen people in a class. By taking a light, unthreatening approach she can instruct on improved hygiene and better grooming techniques. Topics like fingernail care, the use of breath sprays, an extra change of socks and run-free stockings are covered. "A person feels better if he or she looks better," observes Cahan.

She prefers sending an invitation to each employee to attend a class rather than making it appear to be a command. Cahan also recommends having some refreshments for attendees during a short class break.

After the initial training, it's important to have some follow-up. For this Cahan says you can train the trainer. Some excellent department managers may not be good trainers. In those instances, an assistant can be trained. Later, the consultant comes back to do an evaluation and perhaps a review. Training must be an ongoing effort because of employee turnover.

The environment for face-to-face contact

People are sensitive to air temperature, lighting, room decor, comfortable chairs and furniture, plants, flowers and the general appearance of the facility where business is conducted.

Obviously, there is a great diversity in what constitutes the workplace and the environment where customers or clients are met.

Your place of business may be an office, a supermarket, a bank floor, a department store, an airport. Wherever you or company representatives meet *your* public, the proper environment can make the meeting more comfortable, pleasant and often more profitable.

For example, one consultant reports that mirrors have been used effectively to cut down on customer irritability when they must wait for service. He mentions that when tall buildings were first served by elevators the ride was slow. Someone thought to line the elevator walls with mirrors. Complaints about the slow ride dropped markedly. A full wall of mirrors behind a store counter, for example, can have a similar effect. People tend to primp when facing mirrors.

When you meet and greet customers in an environment you control, you have an opportunity to influence the background of where the action takes place.

9

Your Business Clothes Can Do a Lot for You

Your personal feeling may be that the business look is just for executives who are clothes conscious. In reality, this is not so. Even executives who have no personal desire to dress up for business often form their first impression of others based on their clothing, accessories and grooming. What else do you have to go on in those first few impressionable seconds when you meet someone? Remember, first impressions are difficult to change.

Some executives assume that if their clothing and accessories are expensive, they're automatically dressed correctly. This is not always the case. Clothing and accessories used to project a businesslike image have two functions:

1. To help you make a statement about yourself.
2. To indicate that you fit in with the environment in which you are functioning.

An executive who wears a silk suit or a blazer with an ascot is saying something. So, too, is the executive who wears a tie, sports jacket and trousers whose colors clash. The clash is obviously intentional and is often accompanied by eyeglass frames that were stylish in the 1930s and a haircut that is disheveled. A silk suit or ascot leaves an impression of success; the clashing wardrobe may say, "I'm creative, eccentric and do things my way." Nevertheless, the jacket and tie say, "I'll go along with you to a certain extent." An outfit cannot be judged by itself.

One must be aware of its function before passing judgment on it. Obviously, some executives can get away with more than others due to their reputations or because their areas of expertise allow them to affect a nontraditional style of clothing.

In general, most people prefer to deal with executives who are successful. Assuming one is successful, he or she is accustomed to the finer things in life, which supposedly include expensive, well-tailored clothes and accessories. But the fact is that an executive's clothes can have the right look without costing a bundle. The color, material, fit and style of clothing are vital when clothing is used to make a statement. Expensive clothes that are wrinkled, fit poorly, or are not in acceptable colors for business make the wrong statement.

The first impression is vital

"Don't judge a book by its cover" and "Beauty is only skin deep" are adages that are usually not heeded in the business world. If something about an executive turns you off, chances are you'll never get to know more about him or her. What's more, once that first impression is formed, it takes a lot to alter it. Almost everyone would agree that one's clothing alone is not enough. But before a single word is said, your eyes are making judgments which form that first vital impression. It is often lasting.

How to use clothes, accessories and grooming to make a positive statement

The first thing to determine is exactly what statement you want to make. But no matter what the statement, this checklist should be adhered to:
- Hair should be neatly combed and clean.
- Shoes should have a well-polished look.
- Jackets that are skimpy should be avoided.

- A man's tie should end just above the belt.
- Suit material should not be 100% polyester.
- The most acceptable business colors for suits are gray and blue.
- Ideally, a tie should be made of silk.
- Women's blouses should be made of either silk or silklike polyester, or cotton. For a conservative statement, the best colors are white or off-white.
- A man's shirt collar should be large enough to be buttoned comfortably and worn with a tie.
- Jewelry should not be obtrusive.
- A white shirt is preferable as an accessory to a suit.
- Avoid colognes, scented powders and perfumes during business hours.

Pay attention to local customs regarding clothes

What's "in" in New York may be "out" in West Coast cities or smaller cities and towns. If in doubt about local customs, it is better to be overdressed than underdressed. In some areas it is difficult to tell who's who by judging individuals' clothing. In most cities, however, you can spot the higher-ranking executives by the clothes they wear. This is especially so with regard to women executives and their female secretaries. If the custom is for secretaries to wear skirts and blouses, usually the female executives wear suits. In some areas the customs changed and secretaries began wearing suits. Women executives then countered and switched to dresses.

Sexy clothes are a "no-no"

Conventional restrictions on men's wardrobes make it difficult for them to wear sexy outfits. But women executives should be careful not to wear items of clothing that may be inappropriate. A dress in lieu of a suit may be fine if the dress is businesslike and not a revealing outfit better suited for a cocktail party. See-through blouses, tight garments, revealing slits in skirts and low-cut dresses are not considered proper business attire. More often than not, they will backfire on the executives who wear them.

Props also make a statement

A briefcase, notepad, or even a pen in your hand makes a statement. You're saying, "I'm here to conduct business." If you make these props evident after some initial small talk, you will usually move more quickly into business talk. If you pull files from your briefcase and set them out before they are mentioned, you are signaling the start of a business conversation. Also, when arriving for an appointment, if you are carrying a briefcase it is clear that you are on a business mission.

Props should follow the tenor of the rest of your clothing:

- The briefcase should be made of leather. It's fine if the leather looks somewhat worn as long as the briefcase is not falling apart.
- The pen should be silver or gold.
- Any other props must be of visibly high quality in keeping with the rest of your clothes.

Try to avoid colognes and other fragrances

You have everything to gain and little to lose by avoiding personal fragrances. Those who use fragrant powders and wear colognes can easily offend one or more persons in elevators or meeting rooms with poor air circulation. The negative reaction to these fragrances isn't worth the risk. A large number of people are allergic to ingredients used to manufacture powders, colognes and the like. Generally, these people will go out of their way to keep someone who offends them out of their presence. Some executives have been using expensive cigars as a prop for years. They, too, should be mindful that some people find cigar smoke offensive.

Powerful clothing and props are subtle, not garish

No matter what your clothing or props, do not let them "shout" at people. They should be kept simple and somewhat inconspicuous. Don't do anything to call attention to them. They will do their job and be noticed even if partially hidden. Reference should never be made to clothes or props. If, during the course of a meeting, an item is noticed and commented upon favorably, a simple "Thank you" is the best reaction. It is proper for you to commend someone on his or her clothes or accessories if you feel genuine about it, but avoid doing so immediately after you receive a compliment. When complimenting someone on his or her clothing or jewelry, do not ask where the person bought it or if it is new. This information will be offered by the person complimented if it is his or her desire to do so.

Etiquette regarding wearing apparel

- If you or someone in your party is wearing an expensive fur garment, do not offer to check it in a restaurant. Doing so will cause the owner of the garment to feel uncomfortable and also might alarm the checkroom attendant. If others are checking their garments, say, "I assume you'd rather keep your coat with you." Then you can help the person remove the coat. Once shown to your table, place the coat or jacket behind the chair of the person who owns it. If the maitre d' offers to take the coat (in many fine restaurants, checking furs is routine), defer to the owner's wishes.
- When in a meeting, do not remove your suit jacket

or loosen your tie unless the host or hostess does so or suggests that everyone do so.

- As a guest in someone's office, do not remove your suit jacket, even if the person you're visiting has his or her jacket removed. If the person you're visiting asks if you would like to remove your jacket, it is proper to do so, but not mandatory.

- If you are in shirtsleeves in someone's office, never roll up your sleeves, even if others do.

- Upon entering an office, if a receptionist or secretary offers to take your outer garment, it is proper to accept.

- It is not proper to fold your coat or other apparel onto a visitor's chair in someone's office unless you're told to do so.

- Do not place your briefcase on a chair or desk. Keep it on your lap or on the floor beside you.

- It is not proper to comb your hair or apply makeup in someone's office. If necessary, excuse yourself and take care of your grooming in a restroom.

- If you need a place to rest a file, do not move items on someone's desk to make room for it. Use your lap.

- When inclement weather has you wearing overshoes or carrying a wet umbrella, check with a receptionist or secretary for a place to store them before entering someone's office.

10

Proper Etiquette Leads the Way
to Personal Confidence

Lack of confidence often gets in the way of an executive's performance and advancement. Sometimes a poor self-image can cause an executive to shy away from a conversation, invitation or other activity that would be in the executive's best interest.

The degree of an executive's confidence shows itself repeatedly. People gauge an executive by the amount of confidence he or she displays. It is one of the measuring sticks used to size up an executive. What's more, confidence is not entirely a matter of appearing cool, calm and collected. Lack of personal confidence, or a poor self-image, is difficult to cover up by merely acting confident. The feeling has to be genuine and come from within, or it is not usually projected to others.

In this sense, "the clothes make the man" has some degree of validity. It is true that clothes and accessories often help an executive feel right about himself or herself. This genuine feeling is projected to others in the executive's presence.

There are many things an executive can do to boost his or her self-image and confidence. These methods fall into the category of proper etiquette.

Good grooming makes you feel good about yourself

When you take a look at yourself in the mirror and you like what you see, it improves your self-confidence to a large extent. If your hairstyle or your clothing makes you look good and contributes to the image you want to express or how you feel about yourself, it will add to your confidence. Whether or not you receive compliments on your hairstyle or clothing is not important. If you like them, you're happy to be seen and will automatically act accordingly without putting on an act.

Your clothing can add to your confidence

Imagine how you might feel if you were dressed in jeans at a formal event where everyone was dressed in formal clothes. More than likely you would want to hide. The opposite holds true when you are dressed properly with clothing and accessories that you feel portray your position and personality to perfection. Under these conditions, your self-image is bolstered and you want to be seen.

Manners play an important role in boosting confidence

When you walk into a situation and are positive you know how to handle yourself, your self-confidence is projected to everyone in your presence. When it comes time to make an introduction, or engage someone in conversation, you are smooth and personable, clearly a person people admire and enjoy knowing.

You can correct most hang-ups that bother you

Some executives break into a sweat if they know they'll be meeting a lot of people or speaking to a large group.

As they speak they have to wipe the perspiration from their faces. They fear the perspiration will come through their shirts, dresses and jackets. Excessive perspiration is a common trait when people are nervous. You might be surprised to find out that a person you admire has the same problem. But you can be sure that he or she does something about it.

Practice makes perfect

If you are concerned about something like making introductions, and perhaps feel clumsy when greeting people, practice in front of a mirror. Experience leads to perfection. Watch yourself in a mirror as you introduce imaginary people out loud. You can even tape yourself and then listen carefully for intonations, word usage or other things you may want to improve. You'll find that the experience you gain in this way will give you confidence and poise for the real thing.

Make a mental note of what you'll be doing

Before attending an event that makes you feel uneasy, rehearse your actions in your mind. Picture yourself making proper introductions, shaking hands, and opening conversations. This method, called visualization, has proved itself for athletes. Skiers, gymnasts, baseball and football players, for example, often find it helps them immeasurably to rehearse in their minds what they want to do on the field. You can do the same thing.

Maintain a healthy stride and good posture

Good posture and a healthy stride do more than help you breathe better. They say something about you. The image of an executive who walks into a room at a good clip, with head erect and shoulders back, sets the stage for everything else he or she will do to boost both self-image and the image projected to others. Once the stage is set, it's far easier for others to expect and accept the poise and confidence that follows.

Overcome self-doubts and accept yourself

If you have a light complexion and are short, you may never be able to be tall, dark and handsome, but you can be a leading man. If you're not "36, 24, 36," you may never be a sex symbol, but you can be a leading lady. There are some things we can't change. But one thing is for sure: We can use most of what we're born with to our advantage. Today's leading men in motion pictures, the ones who always wind up with the gal, are often barely five feet tall with features probably no better than yours. The same holds true for today's leading ladies who wind up with the guy. Some of them are not nearly as good looking as the average woman on the street. These people project a personality, a sense of being that overcomes their size and features. And they are accepted as they wish to be. You can do the same. In a business setting, proper etiquette and protocol, performed smoothly, are the answer.

As you can see, business etiquette and protocol are a two-way street. They do as much for you, personally, as for the person on the receiving end of your fine manners and refined ways.

If you're engaged in selling a product or service, or moving up the executive ladder, you must be in a position to sell yourself first. What people don't realize is that they must be sold on themselves before they can do a good job of selling themselves to others. Fine-tuning one's skills in business etiquette and protocol is one of the most important ways to increase your self-image and project your confidence to others.

11

Playing by a Different
Set of Rules:
Doing Business with
Executives
from Foreign Lands

When executives travel abroad to engage in business, they can't automatically fall back on the standards, practices, rules and routines they normally engage in at home.

There are numerous stories of blunders that surround American business ventures in foreign countries. Some misunderstandings are due merely to poorly translated terms and phrases, especially in advertising campaigns. But many are the result of not understanding cultural differences.

Since good business manners are expressed in verbal and written communications, it is essential that careful attention also be given to language translation.

No doubt you will turn to professional translators to accomplish the job. But you can also set up a network of fail-safe measures to back up even the most competent translator.

- *Give it time.* Plan assignments in advance so the translator can bring creativity to the assignment. This is often necessary when a literal translation may be inappropriate.
- *There's more than meets the eye.* Let your translator have more to work with than the written message. Tell him or her something about the purpose of the message and the people who will receive it.
- *Get a second opinion.* A local translator should review the finished communications. Trendy words

and phrases change frequently. What is acceptable in one region of a country may not be appropriate elsewhere. A local translator can oversee the sense of the message.

Creating business letters, invitations and thank-you notes in a foreign language takes considerable effort, but the impact of your effort is not lost on the recipient. Of course, if the other party has a good command of your language, it may be better to avoid translation.

Speech . . . speech

If your foreign business hosts speak your language well, you might still choose to learn a few phrases in their language before you travel abroad. These can be used in a speech made to a group, or as you are introduced to others on a one-to-one basis. This is a gracious gesture and may be well received by those you would like to impress. It is important, however, to use the right phrases and pronounce them correctly. A short phrase or two should be delivered almost as though you were a native. Check with an expert. (A phone call, for example, to a tourist bureau office can confirm or correct your pronunciation and selection of words.)

Patterns and practices

You may be surprised to find that some people you meet stand especially close to you when they speak. Others invite you for a meeting, then avoid your attempts to talk about business.

The list of behavior practices and patterns that may confront you in different international settings can be lengthy. Since you have to keep business goals uppermost in your thoughts, it makes sense to get as much information as you can about the people and place(s) you are going to visit well in advance of your trip. This will make you more comfortable when doing business abroad. For example, if you've done your homework well, you will avoid the inconveniences of arriving during a special festival period when many business offices are closed and streets are crowded, or when religious obligations make your contacts unavailable. Time spent gathering or updating this kind of information beforehand may prove invaluable. Here is a potpourri of practices and patterns:

- A South American businessperson is likely to stand closer to you than a North American colleague when the two of you engage in face-to-face, stand-up conversation.

- Scandinavians may feel that you stand closer to them than their colleagues would.

- Although you have been invited to attend a business meeting, it may not begin until some refreshments have been offered. In the Middle East and Northern Africa, a dark coffee or tea is served. It would be a social blunder to refuse the beverage.

- French businesspeople rarely, if ever, invite a business visitor to their home to dine. When taking business guests to a restaurant, the French host may take charge of ordering the meal and wine without asking the guest to make any decisions.

- Evening meals are taken at a late hour in many countries. Nine or ten o'clock is not unusual.

- In Germany and the Netherlands, visiting business guests may be invited home to lengthy dinners which include numerous courses. Hospitality may be demonstrated by urging the guest to consume great quantities of food.

- In India, the dinner may be exotic with foods that include spices.

- In many Japanese homes and business places, shoes are removed and slippers may be supplied. Be alert to this practice. It is best to follow the example set by your hosts.

- When visitors are permitted to enter an Islamic mosque, they must remove their shoes.

- In a Moslem household, alcohol is seldom served. And it may be inappropriate to smoke.

- When you are a guest at a home in Israel, the rules of kashruth may be observed. You would not be served milk and meat at the same meal. If you partake of meat, milk will not be served with coffee nor butter with bread.

- Siesta time is still observed in some Latin countries. Stores may close from about 1 P.M. until 4 P.M. and may remain open until 8 P.M.

- In countries where a siesta time is observed, banks or other establishments may be open for business in the earlier part of the day only.

- Fridays and Saturdays, as well as Sundays, are days when the Sabbath is observed in some countries. Furthermore, some countries' diverse populations result in the official observance of each of the three days. As a result, it may not be possible to conduct business for longer than four days a week.

- Ramadan, a thirty-day period of fasting between dawn and dark, can slow down business transactions with observing Moslems. The traveler must be certain to check a current calendar, since this period does not come at the same time each year on our calendar.

- Public transportation may be unavailable in some countries during the Sabbath hours.

This brief sampling of patterns and practices suggests that the business traveler not only should be well-informed before initiating a trip, but also should spend time considering how to handle some situations.

No matter how reliable your source of information, it is important to remember that most information is somewhat generalized. For example, a shopping mall in your home community may not have business hours on Sundays. A foreign visitor might mistakenly interpret that to mean that all small town shopping malls are closed on Sundays. Keeping this example in mind, when you travel abroad you should be ready for surprises.

Gift-giving customs

The Parker Pen Company once funded a study of more than 125 international business executives who averaged 18 years of foreign travel. The following business gift-giving pointers emanate from the study:

Japan

- You may receive a gift when you first meet a Japanese businessman. You need not reciprocate immediately, but it is acceptable to do so, if you prefer. However, don't surprise a Japanese person with a gift. He may feel uncomfortable about not having something for you.
- Unless you are prepared to give gifts to everyone assembled, wait until you are alone with the recipient before you present a gift.
- Always bring a gift when visiting a home.
- Colors have special meanings to the Japanese. Red is associated with healing and well-being. Black and white are reserved for funerals.

Europe

- Gifts for children are especially appropriate.
- When invited to someone's home for dinner, plan to have flowers delivered. Although you may bring them, it's preferable to send them.

- Be aware that red roses and white flowers, even numbers, and the number 13 should be avoided. (Ask the local flower vendor for assistance when making the selection.)
- Gift wrap should be simple.

The Arab Countries

- Don't give a gift for a wife or wives. (It may even be impolite to ask about your host's wife.)
- Something to be used at the office is an appropriate gift.
- Liquor would not make an appropriate gift.
- A gift presented at your first meeting with someone may be misunderstood.
- Avoid items that depict animals or animal sculptures. Some are symbols of bad luck.
- If you openly admire an object, your host may feel obligated to make it a gift to you.

Latin America

- Avoid black and purple colors and the number 13 when choosing a gift.
- Gifts shouldn't be presented at the same time business is to be conducted. Since no business will be discussed during lunch, this is a proper time to present a small gift.
- The latest in toys will please both children and parents.
- Gifts from female executives to male executives may be open to misinterpretation.

- Some limited gift-giving is practiced. However, never make an issue of a public or private presentation of a gift.
- Small mementos are appreciated.
- Never give a clock as a gift. The word for clock in Chinese sounds like the Chinese word for funeral.
- All business negotiations should be completed before a gift is presented.
- Offer a good reason for presenting the gift. The recipient can use it to justify accepting it.

When you're doing business away from home, you need all the help you can get to avoid turning a well-meaning gesture into a major affront. Here, too, generalizations may prove risky. Try to get input from more than one source. Bear in mind that businesspeople from foreign lands may act differently when doing business with you in the United States than they would when you visit them in their homeland.

12

Proper Protocol Associated
with
Large Meetings

Large meetings tend to be more formal than smaller ones. Somehow, when more than fifteen or twenty people gather in a room, those in attendance have different expectations of how the meeting should take place. A microphone is introduced. There's usually a more formal agenda. The chairperson's role becomes more critical in maintaining a sense of order. And there is a greater adherence to the rules of etiquette and good form.

There are seven steps of protocol that should be adhered to at large meetings:

1. *Flags:* The flag of the United States must be placed to the right of the speaker, or the left of the audience. State flags and company emblems should be placed to the left of the speaker, or the right of the audience. The flag should not be used for any purpose other than displaying it from a staff or across the wall behind a speaker. When displayed on the wall, the union (field of stars) should be uppermost and to the left when viewed. All in attendance should rise and stand quietly at attention during the salute to the flag and during the playing of our national anthem. Civilians place their right hands over their hearts when saluting the flag.

2. *Greeting guests:* The chairperson of the meeting, or someone he or she has designated, should stand ready to greet guests who may not know others

attending the meeting. The greeters should make some introductions and see to it that the guest is comfortable. If drinks are being served, the greeter should offer a drink to the guest. The greeter's job is done once the guest is engaged in conversation with one or more attendees and is obviously at ease.

3. *Seating arrangements:* If there is a head table, it is best to plan well in advance who will sit at it. Be careful not to overlook someone who might feel offended if not invited to sit at the head table. Generally, the guest, chairperson, and other speakers are seated at the head table. When it's necessary to fill out the head table with other people, there's a danger of upsetting someone who is of equal rank to the person seated in a place of honor.

4. *Waiting for latecomers:* It is not in good taste to delay the start of a meeting for more than a few minutes. Unless the speaker is unavoidably delayed, or a dignitary is late, do not wait more than ten minutes to begin.

5. *Avoiding arguments and disagreements:* A large meeting is usually not the right forum for major disagreements and debates. It is the chairperson's responsibility to put an end to debates tactfully, either by citing *Robert's Rules of Order* or offering a different forum for taking up the matter.

6. *Acknowledging guests and dignitaries:* Proper protocol requires that everyone at the head table be acknowledged. When guests and dignitaries are visitors, obtain a brief biography of each person and compose proper acknowledgments and introductory remarks. A person should be assigned to make the introductions. The order of introduction, if there is more than one person speaking, should also be decided in advance. Dignitaries

should always be addressed by their titles from the head table.

7. *Ending the meeting:* It is the responsibility of the chairperson to end the meeting on time. In lieu of an official chairperson, whoever calls the meeting is responsible for ending it.

13

Polished In-Person Greetings and Introductions

The main rule of good manners in greeting people and making introductions is to be considerate of everyone you encounter. Even if you don't know the precise rule at a particular time, if you put someone at ease and show proper respect for that person, you can be sure that your actions are proper. There are times, though, when an encounter requires greetings and introductions for which there are established approaches. Knowing how to handle these kinds of situations will make you more comfortable and will help you create a more gracious atmosphere.

The handshake

When to extend your hand:

- On meeting someone for the first time.
- On greeting someone you haven't seen for a while.
- On saying hello to your host or hostess at a party— or to greet your guests at your party.
- On saying your good-byes to people other than your colleagues when leaving a gathering.

A proper handshake:

- The handshake should be firm, but not a bone-breaker.
- The hand may be "pumped" once or twice.
- Do not continue to hold on to the hand after shaking

it; even if your introduction continues, the hand should be released.

- Lean forward slightly when engaging in a handshake, smile and make eye contact.
- One usually shakes hands while verbalizing a response to an introduction like, "I am happy to meet you." Greetings like, "Jim has told me a great deal about you," are not in order unless you have genuine reason to say so and the statement makes sense to the person you're meeting (such as the spouse of an executive you have worked with for years and you truly feel that you almost know the person from conversations about him or her).

Hugging, kissing and touching:

- In a business atmosphere, hugging, kissing and touching are strictly taboo.
- It is not polite to put an arm around colleagues of the opposite sex, place your hand on their shoulder, or touch them in any other way, no matter how close you might feel to them.
- Kissing should be reserved for when you first meet your spouse at a business gathering.

Making the introduction

When you are introducing one person to another, refrain from long remarks on how you met, or the person's background. A brief point of reference is fine, such as, "Pat Edwards, I'd like to introduce you to Jim Tabors, who is a close friend of mine." As they shake hands, you can say, "Pat is an old schoolmate of mine." Depending on where you are, you can then direct both individuals to a table, lead them to the bar, and so forth. If you are about to excuse yourself, make certain each person is comfortable. When introduced to each other some people fall right into a conversation. If this does not happen, direct the conversation and excuse yourself once the conversation is rolling with both individuals at ease.

- If no one introduces you, wait about five seconds, then approach the party and introduce yourself. Do not say, "We weren't introduced," and avoid asking for an introduction. If appropriate, extend your hand, smile, lean toward the person slightly and say something like, "I'm Bill Smith, Fred's attorney." Avoid phrases of superiority like, "Jack works for me," or "Herb is my foreman." Instead say, "Jack and I work in the same department."

- If you forget the name of someone you're introducing, it's best to be honest and ask the parties to introduce themselves to each other as follows, "I'm terrible with names today, why don't you introduce yourselves." After introductions are made, you can refer to each person as long as the reference is legitimate. Don't say, "Jim is my best friend," when you can't remember his name. But you can say, "I'm glad you have the chance to meet each other; you have a gardening interest in common."

- When you introduce an older person to a youngster, use the youngster's full name and the older person's last name. "Mr. Jones, I would like you to meet Nancy Smith."

- Anyone who appears to be under the age of thirty should be introduced to someone appearing fifteen or more years older with the first and last name of the younger person and Mr., Mrs., or Ms. and the last name of the older. It is up to the individual to ask that he or she be addressed by the first name.

- It is respectful to address the older person, guest of honor or dignitary first when making an introduction.

- A man is always introduced to a woman: "Ms. Jones, I would like you to meet Mr. Smith."

- A youngster is always introduced to an adult: "Mr. King, I would like you to meet my daughter, Janice White."
- If someone pronounces your name incorrectly, it is proper to give the correct pronunciation when acknowledging the person to whom you are being introduced.
- It is permissible to introduce people by just stating their names: "Ms. Smith, Bob Jones," but adding an introductory phrase is preferable.

14

The Consummate Executive Diplomat

Diplomacy, which falls into the areas of etiquette and protocol, is by no means limited to members of foreign services. Executives who sharpen their skills in diplomacy have a tool working for them that puts them at a great advantage. It enables them to say no to something without closing the door on it or uttering a quotable remark they would rather avoid. It lets them agree to something, in spirit, without being bound to the agreement. It gives them the means of pointing a finger at someone, or criticizing something, without mentioning names or incidents. It allows executives to make comments that they can disclaim, if necessary.

The purposes behind diplomacy are not disseminating falsehoods or running a smear campaign against someone. Executives are often bound by decisions made at a higher level. When questioned about these decisions, they are placed in the difficult position of upholding the decision, but not prostituting themselves. In these cases, diplomacy can be a way out for them.

Sometimes, an executive might find it in his or her best interest to soften the blow of criticism that must be made. Or, he or she is not at liberty to make a statement that is to be formally announced by a colleague. Moreover, there are times when an executive is chosen to make a statement on behalf of the company, and wants to distance himself or herself from it personally. These, too, are times when the skillful use of diplomacy gives an executive a special advantage.

Diplomacy constitutes more than words alone. It includes one's mannerisms, demeanor, attitude and timing as well.

Key phrases used in diplomacy

Executives learn early in their careers that it is not usually wise to say precisely what comes to mind under certain conditions. When confronted by salespeople, associates, colleagues, suppliers and the media, a diplomatic answer is often the best approach. Here are some situations and the diplomatic phrases to handle them:

The sordid details

- A colleague questions, "Did you hear about the affair the boss is having with Judy?"

(You feel like saying, "Why don't you mind your own business?")

The Diplomatic Answer: "No. I don't pay attention to those kinds of rumors."

Reacting to a rumor

- An employee confronts you with the statement, "Is it true that thirty-five people will be furloughed soon?"

(You want to say, "Yes. It was decided at a meeting this morning and will be announced on Friday.")

The Diplomatic Answer: "Personnel matters that relate to the company as a whole are announced by our Personnel Department. I'm really not the right person to ask."

Criticizing on request

- At a meeting, you are asked to give your point of view about someone's idea.

(You believe the idea in question is not in the company's best interest and don't want to endorse it.)

The Diplomatic Answer: "It may be that parts of Jim's idea can be used with a more comprehensive approach to the problem of...."

Reacting to a supplier's concerns

- A supplier queries, "Jane told me that you are about to discontinue your XYZ line. Is it true?"

(You want to say, "Probably. A final decision will be made in three months.")

The Diplomatic Answer: "All of our lines come under review routinely. There has been no decision to discontinue the XYZ line, or any other of our lines for that matter."

Dealing with a salesperson

- A salesperson asks, "Isn't this product the best one that is available for your needs?"

(You want to say, "There may be a better one. We're checking it out now. I hate it when you try to ram your wares down my throat.")

The Diplomatic Answer: "Your product seems to answer our needs. However, we will not be making a decision today. Since I'm sure you agree that your product sells itself, we will appreciate your patience in waiting for a reply until we're ready to give one."

Responding to a reporter's questions

- A reporter calls on the telephone and asks, "Is it true that John Smith is about to resign from your company?"

(The fact is John Smith is resigning and the details of announcing his resignation are currently being worked out.)

The Diplomatic Answer: "As a matter of policy, I never comment on rumors, especially when they involve personnel matters."

- The reporter then asks, "Will you deny Smith is about to resign?"

The Diplomatic Answer: "As I said, as a matter of policy I never comment on these matters."

Note: Do not use the phrase "I will neither confirm nor deny..." unless you want to send a message that Smith is about to resign.

When you don't agree with the decision

- You are called upon to expound on a company decision.

(The fact is that you disagree with the decision, yet it has been approved.)

The Diplomatic Answer: "We believe the new program we are initiating will do the job for which it is intended."

- If asked how you feel personally about the project.

The Diplomatic Answer: "Executives in our company work as a team. It is our team effort that is behind much of our success. Once a decision is made, we all stand behind it. Stating personal feelings is counterproductive to, and not in the best interests of, the team spirit for which our company is known."

There are additional diplomatic phrases that can be used:

To point a finger at someone

"I don't believe that we gain anything when one of our executives compromises our meetings by revealing privileged information discussed among us."

To point a finger at something

"Sales pirated from one department to another do not constitute greater profits, any more than switching money from one pocket to another makes a person richer."

To kill a topic of conversation

"I don't believe this is the most opportune time to take up this matter. Let's give it every advantage by discussing it at a more productive time."

Diplomacy beyond words

Body language also plays an important role in diplomacy. It isn't always what you say that counts, but how you say it. A smile or frown that accompanies the same words can make different statements. The stress placed on words can emphasize them. The timing of your speech can put greater weight on key phrases. And you can further accentuate your message with hand gestures.

Starting off a conversation with an amusing remark can dilute the severity of what you are about to say. Introducing a statement with a serious remark about it can amplify its importance.

117

15

Gratuities: When and How Much?

In our society tipping is an accepted tradition. Although a tip is supposed to be given for extra attentiveness, courtesy and extraordinary service, you are almost forced to tip handsomely in a business setting. Convention makes it pretty much an obligation. In fact, even if you have good reason not to tip, you might cause your guests to feel embarrassed or, at the least, uncomfortable if you don't. Refusing to tip is tantamount to making a scene. And that's the last thing you want to do when hosting a business luncheon or dinner.

So though it is acceptable, in terms of etiquette, to show your displeasure with someone serving you by not tipping, it would be in bad taste not to tip if it causes your guests to feel uncomfortable. You can, however, adjust the size of a gratuity in keeping with the kind of service you and your guests receive. So, basically the question is not whether to offer a conventional tip, but how much the gratuity should be, and when it should be considered obligatory. Tips need not be exact calculations. You can round them off to the nearest dollar or large coin.

- The waiter or waitress at a restaurant customarily receives 15% of the bill, including tax. If the restaurant is among the best in its location, or service is extraordinary, or you or your guests make special requests, you might consider leaving a 20% gratuity. The tip is left on the tray or in the wallet used to present the bill.

- The captain, who seats you and distributes the menus, should receive a gratuity if he prepares dishes expressly for you or performs a service beyond showing you to your table. When a gratuity is in order, it should be 5% of the bill or five dollars, whichever is greater. The tip is handed to the captain, with a word of thanks, as you exit. If you are a regular customer at the restaurant and are shown to a favorite table and given special courtesies, five dollars should be presented to the captain on every third or fourth visit to the restaurant. If the captain addresses you by name when you enter the restaurant, and puts on a bit of a show for your guests, you might raise the occasional gratuity to ten dollars.

- The bartender should be given 15% of the bar bill if you have drinks at the bar before taking your table. Unfinished drinks should be delivered to your table. You should not have to carry the drinks yourself. The bartender's gratuity should be left at the bar as you leave it, even if you're not paying the bar bill separately.

- The wine steward's gratuity should be 15% of the wine bill if he serves the drinks or makes recommendations. His presence will become evident to you as you begin to leave the restaurant. The tip is handed to him with a word of thanks.

- The minimum tip for checking coats should be one dollar, no matter if it's for one or two coats. Add a dollar for three or four coats.

- Washroom attendants should be given a minimum of fifty cents, or a maximum of one dollar, if they hold towels for you, brush your jacket, or offer colognes, special soaps or other grooming products.

- Strolling musicians, if they play requests for you

or your guests, should receive two to five dollars, depending on how many requests they play. A pianist or organist should receive a minimum of two dollars for playing a request, or if you know for sure that he or she would appreciate a drink, you can arrange for your waiter to deliver one. Do not assume a drink would be appreciated, or try to guess what kind of drink the musician would like.

- Parking attendants should be handed one dollar when they deliver your car. No gratuity is given when they take your car. If the doorman calls a taxi for you, hand the doorman one dollar upon entering the taxi. The doorman is not given a gratuity when you arrive and he holds doors open for you.

When you're someone's guest

As a guest in a restaurant, you shouldn't be involved in tipping unless you are checking your coat or ordering your car on your own. Never offer to leave the tip, and don't comment if you believe the tip is too small or too large.

When you are a guest and your host or hostess is not present, tip as you would conventionally. If you are a guest at a private club and your host will not be present at all times, you might ask him or her in advance whether tipping is customary. If you are told that tipping is not allowed at the club, avoid tipping unless you make a special request of someone, in which case a small gratuity may be presented discreetly. Should your gratuity be refused, do not force the issue. Retrieve it and tell the person that you genuinely appreciate the extra service, and leave it at that. Many private clubs' procedures are to bill their members for services. Never insist on paying under these circumstances.

In hotels, gratuities for food and beverages served to you are the same as covered above. Waiters who deliver room service should receive a gratuity of 15% of the bill, in addition to any service charge for the room service. Chambermaids should be given one dollar per person, per night in a moderately priced hotel, two dollars in an expensive hotel.

In addition, the following tips are in order:

- For a regular haircut, one dollar. A haircut plus shampoo or shave, two dollars.
- At a beauty salon, 15% to the person who attends you. If you are receiving more than one service and additional people attend you, the gratuity should be 20%. It is correct to assume that the gratuity will be shared and can be given to your primary attendant, saying, "Thank you. This is for everyone who attended me."
- For a shoeshine, the tip should be one dollar, a bit more for boots.

The gratuity guidelines presented here are for larger cities. They can be cut down a bit in smaller cities. Proper tipping not only makes your guests feel comfortable, but usually pays off in better service once those you tip get to know you. If you take different people out to dinner in the same city on a regular basis, it is good business practice to become a regular patron at one or more restaurants. Once you're known to the maitre d' or captain and the waiters, you will be made to feel important and be in a position to impress those you take to dinner. Most people are impressed when the maitre d' greets their host by name, ushers the person to a favorite table, asks if he or she will have the usual drink, and provides a tray of hors d'oeuvres. Proper tipping and regular patronization make this possible. Most people who make their living from gratuities know what is expected of them and remember faces, names and other details that are important to those they serve.

Tipping should be carried out quietly. Passing money to the maitre d' or wine steward is easy since you'll find

124

your gratuity will be collected without looking at it or calling any undue attention to you. Your tip should be presented as a sincere effort to show your appreciation and not as a person of higher station rewarding a person of lower standing. It is wise to have lower denomination bills and change on hand when you are the host at a restaurant. Tipping money should be kept in a pocket and handed out without shuffling through a wallet or searching for the appropriate bills or change.

Never give a tip and ask if it's okay. Try to avoid making change when you give a gratuity. It is quite proper to add up the bill, but refrain from making remarks on how expensive or reasonable the cost is. If the bill is delivered on a tray, you should replace it facedown. If it comes in a wallet, insert the money or credit card into the wallet and leave it on the table in front of you.

When you are the host or hostess, your actions should make it clear to those serving you. When asked if you would like cocktails, you can repeat the question to your guests. This will let the maitre d' or captain know that you are to receive the bill. It is proper to motion discreetly to the captain or waiter bringing the bill, or to ask for the bill during the time you and your guests are finishing your coffee. If the bill is laid down in the middle of the table, pick it up at once, but discreetly, without making a statement about it.

In large cities, the practice of setting out enough money to cover the bill and gratuity for the waiter is understood. In smaller cities it's best to pay the bill and leave the tip separately. It is proper to pay the bill and gratuity with a credit card. Most restaurants' credit card slips have spaces for tipping. It is also in good taste to pay the bill with a credit card and tip with cash.

16

Male/Female Protocol
at the Office

Many male and female executives feel uneasy about office protocol. They're not sure what's appropriate. The male often feels he is between the proverbial rock and a hard place. His first inclination may be to open the door for a woman, as he was taught to do. But this kind of action may be in conflict with treating his female counterpart as an equal. His attentiveness to a courtesy that he feels is proper may be resented.

The female executive has her own set of predicaments that often lead to uncomfortable feelings. Should she accept special courtesies just for being a woman? In a business setting she prefers to be treated like anyone else. Is she a nuisance to her male counterparts when approaching a door, entering an elevator or taking off her coat? If she reaches for the door when men are present, is she acting in poor taste? Or, when she allows a male executive to open a door, is she asking for special treatment?

Believe it or not, there are ways to eliminate these kinds of dilemmas. Basically, the resolution of male/female protocol in business can easily be accomplished with The Offer and Refusal Technique and The Understanding Strategy.

The offer and refusal technique

This approach is simple. It works well because everyone involved is put at ease. The male executive continues to offer the kind of manners he was taught and with which he is comfortable. The female executive accepts those gestures that she believes to be proper in a business setting, but gracefully declines attentiveness she would rather do without. For example:

- When approaching a door, the female executive can slow her pace and allow the man to open the door for her or, if she gets to the door first, open it for everyone else. Should a male reach out for the door from behind her, she can say, "Thank you. I've got it."

- Upon entering a meeting room, if she notices the men beginning to rise from their seats, she can acknowledge the show of courtesy with a smile, or say, "Please keep your seats. Thank you."

- When taking off her coat and a man offers to help, she can accept the assistance or say, "Thank you, I can handle it myself."

Most men will immediately respond to the woman's wishes, even if it is counter to their own notions of behavior. If the woman declines politely, most male executives will accept the woman's wishes and make a note of her preferences. This leads to The Understanding Strategy.

The understanding strategy

Most people who know someone's preferences in terms of business protocol are happy to comply with them. Ultimately, male and female executives who attend the same meetings or travel together will observe each other's preferences and comply with them, even though they are not stated outright. In a more formal setting, where many people are present, the male executive might feel obligated to engage in the kind of chivalry he normally avoids. This is understandable. Under these circumstances the female executive can either accept or decline in a gracious manner. In these cases, everyone does what he or she sees fit and no one is made to feel uncomfortable.

There are a few situations that are not covered by the techniques and strategies given.

- When a woman and man are having a business luncheon or dinner, the bill is usually placed in front of the person the waiter believes to be the host or hostess based upon his or her actions. More often than not, the bill will be placed in the middle of the table. If it is placed in front of the man and the woman is paying the bill, she should reach over and take it without comment.

- Executives staying at hotels might be better advised to hold their meetings in public rooms rather than the hotel room. In some instances a suite offers a sitting room, which is certainly suitable as long as each individual is comfortable with the setting. Good manners and protocol require that the person who calls the meeting be considerate of how others might feel about the meeting's location.

- There are still some private business clubs that restrict women. To avoid embarrassment, it is wise to check on this before setting a meeting at a private club whose rules are not known to you, since you may be using it on a reciprocal basis.

- Male executives should try to avoid always favoring a female executive as minutes secretary of a meeting. On the other hand, unless this practice is abused, female executives should not resent the role just because they are female.

- Female and male executives should take turns preparing and serving coffee, unless all concerned prefer otherwise.

- A male executive addressing a female executive as "Honey," "Sweetheart," or "Dear," is engaging in a demeaning practice. It is also in poor taste to place one's arm around a female executive's shoulders. This is not proper in a business setting.

17

When You're Away
from the Office

Perhaps one reason familiarity breeds contempt in business is that individuals tend to reserve their best behavior for outsiders, and become a bit lax with their manners when dealing with people they know well. Using proper manners and showing respect for those you care about, know well and see on a daily basis does not necessarily require you to maintain a formal posture with them. But it is important to recognize that the most well-adjusted people have insecurities and may be quite sensitive to the way you interact with them.

This becomes especially important when an executive leaves the office for a day or more. Different people are sometimes left in charge of certain matters. At other times, they take on responsibilities for one or more particular functions in the absence of the executive who normally handles them. When the executive is away, these associates often feel more vulnerable to criticism of the ways they handle matters that are not their regular responsibilities. This feeling of "open season" for personal criticism is exacerbated when the absent executive calls in to see how things are going and is not mindful of his or her associates' sensitivities.

While away, there are several approaches an executive can take to minimize the undue concerns of others and keep morale at the office high. Basically, these methods fall into the category of business etiquette and protocol.

Set the stage before you leave

You can avoid problems when you are away from the office by defining areas of responsibility before you leave. This eliminates individuals' infighting over who is left in charge of what. It also grants designated people specific temporary roles to fill in your absence, and dictates the circumstances when you are to be called before any action is taken. Obviously, it's impossible to foretell exactly what problems might arise while you're away. But it is possible to cover virtually anything that can happen by categorizing various situations. Here are some key points to follow:

- Do not leave someone in charge who is normally of lower rank than those who would have to report to him or her in your absence.

- If your secretary is a central point where individuals in your area are to report, make it clear to everyone that your secretary is coordinating information but is not in charge of activities.

- Let everyone in your area know whom you are designating to be in charge of what functions in your absence.

- Make it clear under what circumstances you do *not* want action taken in your absence.

- Be specific as to who should get in touch with you when necessary. Many executives prefer being called by their secretaries, who have their itineraries. If this is the case, do not only tell your secretary, but also let everyone hear it from you.

- If you know of specific items that will come up when you are away, inform the person who will be acting on them.

- It is not necessary to reveal the reason for being away, or where you are going.

- If you plan to be in touch with associates by phone, let them know in advance. It is best not to say that

136

you will definitely call, or when you will do so. Keep it conditional: "I might give you a call to see how things are going" shows interest, does not require that you call, and takes the call out of the realm of concern over the person's ability when and if you do get in touch.

Checking in when you're away

Some associates get a little overzealous when a colleague is away. They feel this is a good time to do some office politicking, or overstep their boundaries. Generally, overt and covert activities carried out in the absence of an executive will backfire. By checking into the office, however, you can get wind of this and other activities that you might want to be apprised of before your return. In any case, since responsibilities at the office are yours, regardless of whether or not you are present, it makes sense to check in on occasion. Even when away on vacation, one or two calls a week may be in order. If you've set the stage properly before leaving, your calls ought to be short and give you peace of mind, not lead to hours of work. Here are some pointers for checking in at the office when you're away:

- If you have decided on a central calling place, such as your secretary's office, stick to it.
- Ask if anything important or unusual is going on. Check on mail or memos that might be important. Get any statistics in which you are interested.
- Try to avoid sending messages to another person through your secretary or anyone else, unless a question posed requires a simple yes or no answer. Second-party messages often cause confusion and resentment.
- When it is necessary to call on an associate with a particular problem, do not let it seem as if the person is wasting your time or is inefficient for not handling the problem independently.

- Always end your conversation with a "Thank you," and indicate your appreciation for the associate's concern and for informing you of the matter.

- Avoid questions that take on a cross-examination tone. Bring up the problem and then let the person talk. Try not to interrupt the individual. Hold your questions until after the person has finished giving you the update.

- If the individual has made a mess of things, do not discipline the person over the telephone. Instruct him or her on how best to handle the matter. Otherwise, insist that he or she consult someone else at the office, or let it wait until you return.

- Try to avoid implying that you do not trust the person who is acting in your absence. Remember, your associate is probably feeling extra sensitive about handling your responsibilities.

- Should your secretary or someone else reveal a particular problem, do not try to solve it over the telephone. This is especially true if the problem has anything to do with interpersonal relationships. Create a truce in this case, with the promise that you will take up the matter shortly after your return to the office.

- If a superior, major customer, or client leaves word for you, do not return a message via someone else. Your secretary should let it be known that you are away from the office. If the person says that the matter can wait until your return, fine. However, if it's an emergency situation, you should return the call personally.

- Let it be known to whomever you call that no concern is too unimportant for you to hear about. Do not let others determine what can be set aside for the future. Make those decisions yourself.

18

Where to Find Help When You're Not Sure of Proper Procedure

Executives seem to be paying more attention to business etiquette and protocol than ever before. The number of business etiquette consultants has increased—as have books, seminars and other reference material on this important subject.

The following information may prove extremely useful to you as a source for consultants and reference material.

Consultants

- The *Directory of Personal Image Consultants*, 1991 edition fills 285 pages. Each listing provides in-depth descriptions of services offered, including specialties, teaching techniques and fee schedules. Also included is a bibliography that contains names of self-help books and cassettes. (Fairchild Publications, Book Division, 7 E. 12th Street, New York, NY 10003; $35; 212-741-4000.)

- Gale Research Company's *Consulting and Consulting Organizations Directory* is another reference guide. The Personal Development Section of this directory describes a wide variety of specialties, such as executive training skills and the ability to project warmth, sincerity, and a sense of executive power. Information includes addresses, phone numbers, and principals' names. (Gale Research Co., Inc., Customer Service Dept., 835 Penobscot Bldg., Detroit, MI 48226; $410; 313-961-2242.)

- Letitia Baldrige published two books in 1990, including *Letitia Baldrige's Complete Guide to the New Manners for the '90s*. She is president of Letitia Baldrige Enterprises, Inc., 2339 Massachusetts Avenue, N.W., Washington, DC 20008; 202-328-1626. The Corporate Manners Division provides seminars in the fields of executive communication, business manners and human relations. Ms. Baldrige also consults privately on these subjects.

- Susan Bixler, author of *The Professional Image*, is the founder of the Atlanta-based consulting firm, Professional Image, Inc.; 404-953-1653. The book includes a list of dos and don'ts for presenting a professional image. Her programs stress dressing, grooming and body language. She trains salespeople, sales managers and others in some of America's top corporations. (The Putnam Publishing Group, 200 Madison Avenue, New York, NY 10016; paperback $10.95; 800-631-8571.)

- Laura Darius, president, Corporate Communications Skills, 545 Fifth Avenue, New York, NY 10017 (212-370-9888), offers corporate training programs for middle- and upper-level executives.

- Barbara Aron Cahan, management training consultant, Associated Seminars, 7900 Bayshore Drive, Margate, NJ 08402 (609-822-7502), offers training in courtesy, stress management and interpersonal relations for employees and executives. She has conducted seminars for major hospitals, the U.S. Post Office and major corporations.

- Jane and Bob Handly are co-presidents of Life Plus, 8214 Westchester, Suite 750, Dallas, TX 75225, a consultant and public relations firm that offers programs in customer service and stress management (214-363-1591).

Of general interest

- The 14th Edition of *Emily Post's Etiquette, A Guide To Modern Manners,* by Elizabeth L. Post, has chapters entitled, "Office Protocol" and "Your Professional Life." (Harper Collins, 10 E. 53rd St., New York, NY 10022; $4.50; 212-207-7000.)

- John Robert Powers School (check your telephone directory for locations) offers courses for individuals on social conduct. The focus is on learning how to behave in any social situation. Preparation for job interviews is included in the training. This covers how to dress properly and what to say to prospective employers. Programs are available for both men and women.

- Many stores have departments devoted to helping executives make business gift selections. For example, Neiman-Marcus, Westchester, NY, has a corporate services office (914-428-2000, ext. 2304). Many local stores are likely to have expert staffs, who are well trained and able to coordinate gift needs for the holidays, incentive programs and other occasions.

- Check with your telephone company to determine if training aids you may wish to use for your employees are available. For example, New Jersey Bell, 540 Broad Street, Newark, NJ 07101 (201-649-2841) makes films and programs available, free of charge to its New Jersey customers. One twenty-five-minute film shows how phone mix-ups and poor telephone usage wreak havoc in a business. If a customer has a minimum audience of twenty-five, New Jersey Bell will make a speaker available for some programs. One topic, *Your Voice Is You*, emphasizes the importance of voice in reflecting one's personality on the telephone. Slides and recordings are used. It requests that arrangements be made as far in advance as possible.

- Dealers who supply the notes and paper you use may be able to give you expert advice on what constitutes "paper" etiquette. For example, a stationery manufacturer, Crane, provides its dealers with information that covers the selection of paper, type of printing and proper etiquette for a variety of occasions.

Seminars

- Dun & Bradstreet Business Education Services, P.O. Box 3734, Church Street Station, New York, NY 10008-3734 (212-608-9170), offers many seminars, which are available on or off your premises.
- The American Society for Training and Development, 1640 King St., Box 1443, Alexandria, VA 22313 (703-683-8184), a 27,000 member professional association of trainers, should be able to direct you to your local chapter or provide further information. They maintain an automated database, Member Information Xchange. They are also able to locate trainers who specialize in specific subjects. However, this service, MIX, is provided only to Society members. The 1,500 member New York Chapter of The American Society for Training and Development (718-531-8554) can alert callers to upcoming seminars in the New York area.

The international scene

- The Parker Pen Company's 200-page paperback book, *Do's & Taboos Around The World*, covers protocol, gift-giving and receiving, etiquette, jargon and body language in business situations. For ordering information write to Order Department, John Wiley & Sons, 1 Wiley Drive, Somerset, NJ 08875-1272 (908-469-4400).

- Lufthansa German Airlines offers a 366-page hand-size book, *Business Travel Guide to Europe.* It includes hints to businesspeople on a wide range of subjects like tipping, handshakes, attitudes regarding punctuality, and useful expressions in the language of the land. The book is available, upon request, by writing on your company letterhead to: Lufthansa German Airlines, Dept. UM 12, 750 Lexington Ave., New York, NY 10022.

- Japan Air Lines has a gift service available exclusively to passengers traveling on Japan Air Lines. The nearest JAL office should be able to provide details. With two weeks advance notice, JAL can arrange to have your business cards translated and printed in Japanese and English. (The charge is $30 for 100 cards; you pick them up in Japan.) JAL sells books and tapes that may help you prepare for a business trip. Contact: Japan Air Lines, P.O. Box 7712, Woodside, NY 11377, 212-310-1492.)

19

Checking Your Obligations at a Glance

The following checklists have been prepared to protect executives from accidentally being remiss when they are obligated to act in response to invitations, gifts and other occasions.

Invitations and Acknowledgments

Kind of Invitation	Proper Timing	Kind of Response	More Info On Subject
Formal	24 hours	Handwritten in form of invitation	Chapters 3 and 6
Informal	24 hours	Handwritten note	Chapters 3 and 6
Verbal	24 hours	Via telephone	Chapter 3

Notes

Type	Occasion	Timing	More Information
Bread-and-Butter	Thank you for overnight hospitality	Within three days of leaving	Chapter 6
Congratulations	Promotion Birth of a baby Wedding Receipt of an honor	As soon as you receive the news	Chapter 6

Type	Occasion	Timing	More Information
Condolence	Death in the family of a friend or associate	As soon as you hear the news	Chapter 6

Gifts

Determination	Timing	Response	More Information
Acceptance of	24 hours	Handwritten note	Chapters 5 and 6
Refusal of	Immediately	Handwritten note	Chapter 5

Meetings

Protocol	Action	Responsibility	More Information
Flag placement	Right of speaker	Chairperson	Chapter 12
Greeting guests	Delegated people	Chairperson	Chapters 12 and 13
Awaiting latecomers	Generally, 10 minutes	Chairperson	Chapter 12
Acknowledging guests & others	All seated at head table	Chairperson	Chapter 12
Ending the meeting	On time, as scheduled	Person who called meeting	Chapter 12

Making Introductions

Situation	Action	Example	More Information
People of same rank & age	No long remarks	"Bill Edwards, I'd like you to meet Jim Tabors."	Chapter 13
When you're not introduced	Wait about 5 seconds	"I'm Pam Smith, Fred's attorney."	Chapter 13

Situation	Action	Example	More Information
If you forget names	Be honest	"I'm terrible with names today, why don't you introduce yourselves?"	Chapter 13
Older person to younger person	Younger introduced to elder	"Mr. Jones, I would like you to meet Nancy Smith."	Chapter 13
Man to woman	Man is introduced to woman	"Mrs. Jones, I'd like you to meet Mr. Smith."	Chapter 13

Gratuities

To Whom	Amount	How Presented	More Information
Waiter/waitress	15%	At table	Chapter 15
The Captain	5% or $5, whichever greater for extra service	Handed personally when leaving or added to charge slip	Chapter 15
The Bartender	15% of bar bill	Left at bar as you leave it	Chapter 15
Wine Steward	15% of wine bill	Handed personally when leaving	Chapter 15
Coat Checking	$1 up to 2 coats, $2 up to 4 coats, etc.	When leaving	Chapter 15
Strolling Musicians	$2–$5 only for a request	At time of request	Chapter 15